Luther and His Mother

IAN SIGGINS

A man who speaks ill of women has no
inkling of what his mother did. . . .

Martin Luther

Library of Congress Cataloging in Publication Data

Siggins, Ian D   Kingston.
    Luther and his mother.

    Includes index.
    1. Luther, Martin, 1483–1546.   2. Luder, Margarethe.
I. Title.
BR328.S56   284.1'092'4 [B]   80–2386
ISBN 0–8006–1498–4

8576J80   Printed in the United States of America   1–1498

Contents

Preface

Serendipity is the historian's favorite tool. This book is the result of one of those happy tangents that make the pursuit of history so enjoyable.

I had begun to write an article on a completely different aspect of Luther's life. For want of a less conventional opening, I wrote in the very first sentence: "Martin Luther was the son of Hans Luder and Margarethe ('Hanna') Luder, *née* . . .''; and immediately confronted my first hurdle. I was dimly aware that the biographers had differed about Luther's mother's maiden name—an apparently minor, perhaps trivial, point. Should I simply leave it out? For the sake of thoroughness, I decided to try to resolve the issue, at least to my own satisfaction. That was easier said than done. It turned out, as I peeled back layer after layer of the biographical tradition, that the disagreement was very deeply rooted, and indeed went all the way back to the sixteenth century and to the earliest generation of Luther's encomiasts.

In the process, I also noted with some disquiet that many of the assertions blithely made by the Lives seemed to be attested by no particular authority; and if such claims were chased back through the generations to their first appearance, too often the trail petered out in conjecture.

My original puzzle, however, did prove soluble. I was able to find which of the disputed surnames actually belonged to Hanna Luder. And with that simple fact came a body of information about Hanna's kinsfolk, and young Martin's relationship with them, that threw a new light on Luther's early life, his social outlook, his mother's influence, and his spiritual formation. In place of the brief footnote I had originally envisioned, I had happened upon a number of modest but significant additions and corrections to received tradition. In so thoroughly canvassed a field as Luther biography, this was an unexpected and pleasing outcome; and this book is its fruit.

It begins with a review of the traditional portrait of Hanna Luder, and carefully examines the primary records for what little they say about her. (The chroniclers of our history, of course, have almost all been men; and in those generations when a false propriety did not actively discourage them from writing of the womenfolk, their imagination and interest perhaps did not reach as far as the other half of the populace.) Next, it reviews and resolves the debate about Hanna's maiden name. Then it steps aside to look at a much less technical and more colorful controversy involving Luther's mother—the claim by his detractors that Luther was the demonic offspring of a bathmaid and an incubus, a mysterious nocturnal visitor with red cloak and croaking voice. This will give us opportunity to examine the apocalyptic mode in which so much of early Luther biography, favorable and unfavorable, was written. The fourth chapter describes the social background and attainments of Hanna's family and relates the details of young Martin's important contact with them in the impressionable years of his adolescence. Next, special attention is paid to a deeply significant but overlooked source of religious influence on this sensitive youth: the preaching he heard and the spirituality he imbibed in the circle of his maternal relatives. Finally, and more speculatively, Luther's own mature writings are briefly examined for traces of the abiding influence upon him of his mother Margarethe.

Acknowledgments

I want to thank the following friends and colleagues who helped this book reach completion: for various acts of practical helpfulness—Gary Bisbee, Stephen Boyd, Pamela Chance, Viki Dietrich, Margaret Gilmore, Klaus Lindner, Rex Matthews, and Philip Sellew; for their invaluable comments—Heinz Bluhm, Paula Cooey-Nichols, Mark Edwards, Steven Ozment, Susanna Rodell, Lorraine Siggins, and George Williams. I also gratefully acknowledge the assistance of the librarians of Andover-Harvard Library and the Houghton Library of Harvard University. Parts of this book first appeared in an earlier form in the *Harvard Theological Review*; I acknowledge the willingness of its editor, Helmut Koester, to allow the material to reappear in this expanded form · Much of the book was first delivered orally to the Greater Boston Reformation Colloquium, and I am grateful to its members for their encouragement.

All translations from non-English sources, including the Weimar editions of Luther's writings, are my own.

IAN SIGGINS

1

The Tradition
on Luther's Mother

Biographers have been swift to identify the strong, ambivalent impress on Martin Luther of his father, Hans Luder, but of Luther's mother, Margarethe (or Hanna) Luder, history has told us very little. Martin Luther's personal development, Erik Erikson warns, is "an almost exclusively masculine story."[1]

In contrast, some other great figures in the tradition of Western piety have been unmistakably their mothers' sons. Augustine of Hippo has made his mother, Monica, the most famous Christian parent of them all:

I shall not leave unsaid a single word that my mind can bring forth about your servant, my mother: in the flesh, she brought me to birth in this world; in her heart, she brought me to birth in your eternal light.[2]

Luther compared Monica with the biblical Hannah as a model of faithful motherhood.[3]

All the world knows, too, of the intense formative influence of Susanna Wesley on her son, John:

I hope that you retain the impressions of your education, nor have forgot that the vows of God are upon you. . . . I exhort you, as I am your faithful friend; and I command you, as I am your parent, to use your utmost diligence to make your calling and election sure; to be faithful to your God; and after I have said that, I need not bid you be industrious in your calling.[4]

But in Martin Luther's case, there seems little prospect of tracing the strong maternal hand of a Monica or a Susanna Wesley. What do we know about Luther's mother?

I

According to the biographers, very little is known of Margarethe Luder. We have "only a very shadowy conception," Heinrich Boehmer says, in spite of Spalatin's remark that Martin was her "spit and image."[5] Robert Fife agrees:

In comparison with the vigorous outline which the sources draw of the father, Luther's mother, Margareta Ziegler, presents a very incomplete and pale picture. Luther's friends mention the respect in which the town held her, and their testimony and Luther's own leave the impression that she was industrious, self-denying, and devout. The interest of scribe and apologist in that stern era did not linger on female characterization.[6]

Even Erik Erikson, who is quite ready to offer clinical extrapolations from scant evidence, admits that a "big gap exists here, which only conjecture could fill."[7]

The usual picture of Margarethe Luder is of a small, dark woman of dour temperament, whose idea of song was the dismal ditty:

Mir und dir ist keiner hold,
das is unser beider Schuld.
(No one cares for me and you,
That's my fault, and your fault too!)

Though she had the best intentions in the world, she treated little Martin far too severely, once drawing blood when she beat him for stealing a nut, and thus predisposing him to that timidity which drove him to the monastery. In the manner of her kind, she was extremely superstitious and took steps to appease her wicked neighbor, a witch whose fatal spells she feared for the sake of her children. She bore at least eight, possibly nine, children. In the years of the family's poverty she gathered all the firewood and carried it on her back. In her later years, she became a familiar visitor to Wittenberg, had her portrait painted by Cranach, earned the friendship and respect of Spalatin and Melanchthon, gained a reputation as zealous in prayer, and died in faith in 1531, the recipient of a letter of evangelical comfort from her famous son.

This is a fragmentary picture, at best. Very little has been noted about Margarethe Luder. Our sparse and shadowy picture has been based on a few references in Luther's *Table Talk* and letters; laudatory remarks by Melanchthon, Spalatin, and Schneidewein about her godliness have generally been discounted as polite convention. Accordingly, there seems little basis for challenging Erikson's proposal of "an almost exclusively masculine story."

The primary sources on which the traditional picture of Margarethe Luder is founded are even scantier than some biographers admit, for some inevitable embroidering of these meager materials has occurred. Literary embellishments introduced by one biographer are repeated by the next, not as guesswork but as fact. (This is the case, for instance, for the claim that "at home his mother taught him the Ten Commandments, the Apostles' Creed, the Lord's Prayer, and such simple evangelical hymns as: 'Ein Kinderlein so lobelich,' 'Nun bitten wir den Heiligen Geist,' and 'Christ ist erstanden'."[8] It is not impossible, but it has no factual basis outside a nineteenth-century biographer's imagination.) It will be a brief task to review the documentary basis of the traditional description. Even an exhaustive review will yield only a sketch.

II

Our knowledge of Margarethe Luder's appearance comes, of course, from Lucas Cranach's striking portraits of both parents, painted from life in 1527. The portraits make clear that Martin inherited facial characteristics from both Hans and Margarethe but also that there is a stronger resemblance to his mother. That her swarthy Thuringian mien bespoke a dour temperament is a matter of conjecture. Most biographers have drawn this inference from the snatch of the ditty, "Mir und dir," that Luther himself recalled.[9] But it is just as plausible to conclude (as a few biographers have done) that the ditty is evidence of a cheerful temper, and the couplet a piece of wry, tongue-in-cheek self-deprecation (on the order of "The Miller of Dee" or "Nobody loves me"). What is sure is that Luther remembered his mother's singing about the house, and this gives substance to Erikson's suggestion that "nobody could speak and sing as Luther later did if his mother's voice had not sung to him of some heaven."[10]

It is Luther himself who tells us that his mother's name was "Margaretha,"[11] and the contemporary biographers all use some variant of the name (Margaretha, Margrethe, Margarethe). The *Table Talk* indicates, however, that within the family she was usually called "Hanna."[12] Since "Hanna" is not a common or wonted byname for "Margaretha," it is not clear why she was so styled. Perhaps it was because her father (like a number of other men in her family) was called Hans, or simply because she married a man named Hans; but Luther gives no reason.

There is consensus among descriptions of Hanna Luder that "her anxiety for the highest welfare of her child sometimes led her imperfectly educated conscience to unjustifiable severity in dealing with his faults."[13] This is eagerly accepted as one of the few specific facts we know of Luther's childhood dealings with his mother. It is based on a single recollection which Luther mentioned at table to illustrate his continuing concern to moderate corporal punishments in schooling and discipline. His balanced advice to parents and teachers was Solomon's: "Chastise your child while there is hope, but do not drive his soul to death" (Prov. 19:18). He recalled the bad old days when "schoolteachers [were] as cruel as hangmen," and he himself was beaten fifteen times one morning for having failed to memorize his conjugations and declensions.[14] His counsel on correcting childish peccadilloes was the same. Theft must be discouraged, but with discretion: *puerilia* like orchard forays to steal fruit or nuts should not be too severely punished; the time for a beating is when a child steals money or clothing:

My parents constrained me very strictly, to the point of cowardliness. My mother punished me so much over a single nut that the blood flowed. And with such strict discipline they finally drove me to the monastery, even though they earnestly meant it for my good, but I became too cowardly. They were not able to distinguish between torments and corrections, how they should be tempered. When you give a beating, don't knock the apple off the branch![15]

Elsewhere Luther mentioned a similar incident when he received a beating from his father.[16] These are isolated episodes, the sorts of graphically recalled childhood injustices that most adults bear with them from even the happiest childhoods, but for Luther they do express a perennial concern to find the middle way between laxity and fearfulness, in the home and in the school (and perhaps also in the doctrine of faith) It would be a mistake to draw too close a connection between these incidents and his entry, as a young man, into the religious life; but his parents' sternness poignantly contributed to the pervading sense of conflict and fearfulness that led him finally to seek grace in the cloister.

Another item from the *Table Talk* is the single source of our knowledge of Hanna's belief in witches and spells:

Luther often said many things about bewitching, about asthma and nightmares, and how his mother had been plagued by a neighbor who was a witch, so that she was forced to handle her very circumspectly and politely and to conciliate her, for she had blasted her children so that they shrieked themselves to death.[17]

This woman had cast a fatal spell, using earth and water, on a preacher who had reproved her witchcraft in general terms. There is a temptation for us to regard such credulity as evidence of Hanna's primitive and gullible origins; but the belief in magic was age-old, and the dark and twisted form it took in the delusion of that era knew no boundaries of class or culture. The witchcraft terror was to reach its peak of credence and cruelty in the hundred years after the Reformation; and Dr. Luther himself, who did not disapprove the burning of witches in the town square of Wittenberg, fully shared his mother's conviction about the spellbinders' dire powers:

Then Luther was asked whether such things could even befall the godly, and he answered: "Yes, indeed, our soul is subject to deception; and if it is freed, our body is subject to murder. I myself regard my own illnesses not as natural but as mere bewitchments. But may God free his elect from these sorts of evils!"[18]

A handful of other references by Luther to his mother add little to the picture. We discover that while she was certain enough of the day of Martin's birth, she was uncertain about the year—she told Philipp Melanchthon it was 1484, while Luther himself and his brother Jakob believed it was 1483.[19] His parents' conjugal embrace was proof to Luther of the sanctity of married love, for so "my father slept with my mother and embraced her, just as I do with my wife, and they were still godly people."[20] Our knowledge of the fruit of that union must be pieced together from various letters and remarks: though there have long been genealogies of Luther's lineal descendants,[21] there is no similar listing of the collateral lines, and we do not even know the names of all his brothers and sisters. One entry in the *Table Talk* seems to indicate that Martin had an older brother, since it says that Hans Luder went "with his wife and son" from Möhra to Mansfeld and then Martin was born; but this is certainly an inadvertent error of compilation.[22] The only sibling of whom we know much was Jakob, who was Martin's close companion in childhood (according to their mother's own testimony, as reported by Johannes Schneidewein, Rector of Wittenberg University) and the object of his abiding and heartfelt love in adult life:

There was always such mutual good feeling between the two brothers, she said, that neither of them ever preferred any companion to the other, and neither took delight in any food or any game without the other. In later years, many people here saw between the brothers Dr. Martin Luther and Jakob Luther a constant, by no means feigned love, but a true and heartfelt mutual caring, which was confirmed by the many great services that each of them did for the other.[23]

Jakob was at hand in Mansfeld to care for Hans and Hanna Luder in their last years. Two brothers were lost to the plague shortly after Luther was ordained priest in 1507.[24] A sister, Barbara, died in 1520.[25] Another sister, Dorothea, married and became Dorothea Mackenrot;[26] yet another, Margarethe, became Margarethe Kaufmann.[27] A sister whose name is unknown married a husband named Polner. So we know that Hanna Luder bore four sons and four daughters. The bitter facts of infant mortality in that age suggest that she probably lost other children in infancy. In the years of her prime, Hanna's energies were largely consumed by childbearing and nurture.

Were these years also years of poverty? Luther liked to suggest so: "My father in his youth became a poor miner. My mother carried all her firewood on her back. This is how they brought us up."[28] Another reporter adds the remark, "They assumed heavy labors that these days the world would not tolerate." But as we shall see, there is good reason to suppose that Luther was being more romantic than literal when he stressed the humbleness of his origins. His insistence that he was "a peasant's son," that he sprang from a long line of "real peasants," was usually evoked by scorn at someone's well-meaning suggestion that his fame and success were predictable by the stars or by notable parentage.[29] He had considerable investment in emphasizing his own improbability. In fact, his own childhood experience was of a relatively prosperous family, well-connected and with professional expectations, and of a father who was a magistrate and an entrepreneur. It is true that his father had begun life on a farm, but since rural land in Thuringia passed to the youngest son, Hans had early chosen to make his living in the growth industry of the area, the silver mines of the Annaberg. As to the social standing of Hanna's family, there is a puzzle here which we must shortly try to resolve; but we should perhaps take Luther's remarks about his parents' poverty as the characteristic nostalgia of the upwardly mobile for the bad old days.

In their later years, Hanna and Hans visited their now-famous older son in Wittenberg, though we do not know how often. They were both present, with their daughters, at Philipp Melanchthon's wedding in 1520.[30] And of course they were present again five years later for Martin's wedding to Käthe von Bora.[31] On one later occasion, Hanna was prevented from paying an intended visit to Wittenberg.[32] She probably visited the Black Cloister more often than this, considering Melanchthon's affection for her, and the likelihood that Schneidewein's reminiscences came from the time when, as a teenager in Luther's household, he asked her about Martin's own adolescence: "To those who inquired about the origin of her family, the time of her son's birth, or signs of talent in him as an adolescent, she recalled many memories worthy of note."[33] It is our great frustration that more of these memories were not written down to satisfy our curiosity!

Hanna Luder impressed her son's colleagues with her piety and strength of character. Melanchthon was to say of her:

In his mother Margarethe, Johannes Luder's wife, dwelt not only the virtues befitting an upright married woman, but her modesty, fear of God, and prayerfulness were especially obvious, and other upright women paid her close attention as an example of virtue.[34]

Schneidewein says similarly:

His mother's prudence and virtue were so great that her character seemed to recall Elizabeth, the wife of Zacharias, or some equally saintly and wise woman.[35]

III

Hanna Luder died in Mansfeld, in the care of her son Jakob, on 30 June 1531—just over a year after the death of her husband.[36] As she lay dying, Martin Luther wrote her a letter, as he had done to his father, encouraging her faith in the face of this greatest of obstacles:

Grace and peace in Christ Jesus,
our lord and savior, Amen.

My Mother, whom I love from my heart: I have received a letter from my brother Jakob about your illness, and it certainly gives me deep grief, especially since I cannot be with you in the flesh, as I certainly wish I could. Yet by way of this letter I do come to you bodily; and I will certainly not be away from you in spirit, along with all our family.

I expect that long before this you have been instructed enough in spite of my absence; that you, praise God, have taken in his comforting Word; and that you are supplied with enough people to preach it to you and console you. Yet I want to play my part, too. As is my duty, I acknowledge that I am your child and you are my mother, as the God and creator of us both has made us and bound us to each other. In this way I shall increase the number of your comforters.

First of all, dear Mother, through the grace of God you already know well that your illness is a fatherly, gracious chastisement. It's quite a small one compared with the chastisements he inflicts on the ungodly, indeed often even on his own dear children—one is beheaded, a second burned, a third drowned and so on—so we are all bound to sing: "For thy sake are we killed all the day long; we are counted as sheep for the slaughter." So don't let this illness distress or discourage you; but accept it with thanks as sent by his grace, and recognize that even if it leads to death or the grave it is a slight suffering by comparison with the sufferings of his own dear son, our lord Jesus Christ, who did not suffer for himself, as we must, but suffered for us and our sins.

Secondly, you also know, dear Mother, the real foundation and ground of your salvation, from whom you must seek consolation in this and all troubles—the cornerstone, Jesus Christ. He will not waver or fail us, nor let us sink or perish. For he is the savior: he is called "the savior of all poor sinners," all who are bound in need and death and who depend on him and call on his name.

He says: "Be of good cheer, I have overcome the world." If he has overcome the world, then he has certainly overcome the king of this world with all his power. But what else is that power but death, by which he has made us his subjects and held us captive on account of our sin? But now that death and sin have been overcome, we can listen with happiness and comfort to his sweet words: "Be of good cheer, I have overcome the world."

And we must certainly not doubt that these words are really true—and not only that but we are told to receive this consolation with joy and all thanksgiving. Anyone unwilling to be comforted by these words would be doing a real injustice to the dear comforter, and the greatest dishonor—as if he had not really told us to be of good cheer, or as if it wasn't really true that he had overcome the world. We would just be reestablishing inside ourselves the tyranny of the conquered devil, sin, and death against the dear savior. God preserve us from that!

So let us rejoice now, full of assurance and happiness, and if any thought of sin or death frightens us, we should fight it by lifting up our hearts and saying: "Look, dear soul, what are you doing? Dear death, dear sin, how is it that you are still alive and frightening me? Don't you know you've been overcome? You, death, don't you know you are thoroughly dead? Don't you know the one who says about you: 'I have overcome the world'? I shouldn't listen to your frightening ideas or take any notice of them—rather, take notice of my savior's consoling words: 'Be of good cheer, be of good cheer, I have overcome the world.'

"He is the conqueror, the true champion, who with this word: 'Be of good cheer,' gives me his victory and makes it mine. I will stay with him and hold fast to his words and his consolation. Whether I stay here or go beyond I will live by them—he does not lie to me. You want to deceive me with your terrors and tear me away from such a conqueror and savior with your lying ideas, but they are still lies, just as certainly as it is true that he has overcome you and commanded us to be consoled.

"This is the way St. Paul boasts and defies death's terrors: 'Death is swallowed up in victory. O death, where is thy victory? O hell, where is thy sting?' You are like a wooden replica of death—you can frighten and threaten but you don't have any power to strangle, because your victory, sting and power have been swallowed up in Christ's victory. You can bare your teeth, but you cannot devour, for God has given us the victory through Christ Jesus our lord, to whom be praise and thanks, Amen."

Let your heart be moved, dear Mother, by these sorts of words and thoughts—and otherwise, not by anything. Indeed, be grateful that God has brought you to this knowledge and did not let you stay trapped in popish error, which taught us to trust our own works and the monks' holiness, and to regard our only consolation, our savior, not as a comforter but a hard judge and tyrant, so that we were forced to flee from him to Mary and the saints and to expect no grace or comfort from him.

But now we know otherwise—about the unfathomable goodness and mercy of our heavenly Father, how Jesus Christ is our mediator, mercy seat and bishop before God in heaven, who intercedes for us every day and reconciles all those who believe in him only and call upon him, that he is not a judge or harsh except for those who do not trust him or who reject his consolation and grace, that he is not the one who accuses and threatens us but the one who reconciles us and intercedes for us with his own death and the blood he shed for us, so that we must not be afraid of him but approach him with all confidence and call him "Dear savior, sweet comforter, faithful bishop of our souls," and the like.

As I say, this is the knowledge to which God has graciously called you. You have God's own seal and letter of this—the gospel, baptism, and sacrament you hear preached—so you should have no difficulty or danger. Just be of good comfort, and be joyfully thankful for so great a grace. For "he who has begun in you will also graciously complete it." For we cannot help ourselves in such things: for we cannot do anything against sin, death and the devil by our own works. So another appears in our place and on our behalf who can do it very well; and he gives us his victory and commands us to receive it and not to doubt it. He says: "Be of good cheer; I have overcome the world," and also: "I live, and you will live also, and no one will take your joy from you."

The Father and God of all consolation grant you, through his holy Word and Spirit, a firm, joyful, thankful faith to overcome this and all other troubles happily, and at last to taste and experience that it is the truth when he says: "Be of good cheer; I have overcome the world." And so I commend you, body and soul, to his mercy, Amen. All your children and my Käthe are praying for you. Some of them weep, others say at meals: "Grandmother is very ill." God's grace be with us all, Amen. The Sunday after Ascension, 1531.

Your loving son,
Martin Luther[37]

2

The Disputed Name

The historical record about Margarethe Luder is extremely spare, and the few remarks of her son Martin and his colleagues give us only slender hints. The tenuousness of our information about her is rather touchingly mirrored by the disagreement, stretching over four hundred years, about her maiden name: Was it Ziegler, or was it Lindemann?

From the seventeenth to the nineteenth century, a majority of biographers favored the name Lindemann. About a hundred years ago, the consensus shifted to Ziegler, and it became fashionable to say that her "maiden name was Margaretha Ziegler (not Lindemann, as often given)."[1] Half a century ago, the tide turned back in favor of Lindemann. But proponents of both views have published in every period.

It seems that this confusion, at least, can be resolved, and the origins of the confusion identified. And we shall find that there is more in this question than a mere pedantic argument over a surname. So first, let us review the course of the disagreement.

I

As we saw in chapter 1, the earliest sources of our knowledge give only her first name: Luther himself gives it as "Margaretha," or "Hanna" for short.[2] Melanchthon also gives only her first name in his biographical preface to volume 2 of the Wittenberg edition of Luther's works.[3] Cochlaeus (1549), Eber (1556), Fontaine (1558), and Mathesius (1566) all do the same.[4] The earliest mention of a surname comes on 15 June 1558, in the invitation to the funeral of Luther's nephew and namesake, Martin Luther, an official invitation from the Rector of Wittenberg University. In the university register Luther's mother is said to have been "born into the family of the Lindemanns, a cognate relative of the very distinguished man, Dr. Laurentius Lindemann [a former Rector of the University]."[5]

This ought to constitute excellent evidence for the surname "Lindemann," since the Rector of Wittenberg University in 1558 was the jurist Professor Johannes Schneidewein, who from the age of thirteen had lived in Luther's household and must have known the family relationships well.[6] In spite of this apparently unimpeachable source, however, no less an authority than J. K. F. Knaake, first general editor of the Weimar Edition, believed that it could be explained away, and a better case made for the surname "Ziegler."[7]

Knaake's argument proceeds both negatively and positively. First he explains on rather technical grounds why he thinks that Schneidewein is in fact not saying what he seemed to say, and why he is also skeptical of a second source from the sixteenth century for the Lindemann tradition. Having done so, Knaake then argues positively for placing our trust in the earliest source of the Ziegler tradition, Cyriac Spangenberg, whom he holds to be a reliable witness. Because the outcome has weightier implications than meet the eye, we shall follow Knaake through both parts of his argument.

II

Knaake's negative case rests on a parallel passage from earlier in the same official university register: an entry in 1548, when Kaspar Creutziger was rector, says that Ambrose Reiter's wife Walpurga was "born into the family of the Reinecks." But it goes on to say that her mother was Johann Reineck's sister.[8] In other words, she was "born into the family of the Reinecks" in the sense that "her mother was born a Reineck." Therefore, Knaake contends, we must draw a distinction between *agnate* and *cognate* kinship, and he quotes the *Vocabularius breviloquus* (Strassburg, 1501) as a contemporary authority for assigning the term *agnate* to male descent and *cognate* to female. Since "born into the family of the Reinecks" is plainly a case of matrilinear relationship, so also is "born into the family of the Lindemanns." Luther's mother is so described, according to Knaake, because not she but her mother was born a Lindemann, and she was therefore called "a cognate relative" of Laurentius Lindemann.

From Knaake's point of view, this argument clears the way for what he regards as superior evidence for the surname "Ziegler." But the Reineck case is not a decisive parallel. Both Knaake and the *Vocabularius breviloquus* go considerably beyond normal Latin usage, both medieval and classical, in suggesting that *agnate* and *cognate* are mutually exclusive. It is true that *agnate* is reserved for kinship on the father's side, but *cognate* is everywhere used for kinship on either side, father's as well as mother's. Thus it is perfectly correct, for instance, to define *agnate* as "cognate on the father's side." There is, then, at least a fifty percent chance that the Wittenberg entry, "Lindemann," does after all give Hanna Luder's maiden name.

Knaake's skepticism is also provoked by several difficulties in another sixteenth-century source of the Lindemann tradition, the report of a 1582 statement by Adam Beerwald, pastor and superintendent at Zwickau. Our knowledge of this source comes from the seventeenth century, when V. L. von Seckendorff first tried to resolve the issue of Hanna's surname in his *Commentarius . . de Lutheranismo.*[9] In the eighteenth century W. E. Tentzel, *Bericht . . . der Reformation Lutheri,*[10] explained the documentary basis of von Seckendorff's information in a long footnote. (By then the biographers were already equally divided between "Lindemann" and "Ziegler.") Von Seckendorff's source, according to Tentzel, was a number of letters he had obtained from Görlitz from people he regarded as trustworthy witnesses. The letters told the following story. In 1582, Pastor Beerwald's oldest daughter, Anna, was married to Martin Meinhard, the corector of the parish. On this occasion Beerwald made the customary oration before the nuptial bed, and his remarks were recorded by Wolfgang Silber, then deacon at Hartenstein and later pastor of Greiffenberg and Chemnitz, who was himself to marry Beerwald's other daughter in 1590. In Silber's version, Beerwald said:

My dear wife Salome's father, Johannes Lindemann, belongs to the family of Dr. Martin Luther. Her great-grandfather, who lived in Franconia, had one daughter and three sons. One son moved to Meissen, and his son became Dr. Lindemann at Dresden. The second son was called Cyriac Lindemann, moved to Thuringia and became schoolmaster at Gotha. The third remained in Franconia, and his son is my father-in-law, Johann Lindemann. But Luther's father took to wife the daughter of my father-in-law's grandfather. Thus my father-in-law is kin and cousin of Luther's.[11]

Knaake correctly points out that there are sheer impossibilities in this account. For instance, Cyriac Lindemann did not move from Franconia to Thuringia, but was born in Gotha in 1516, the son of the tailor Hans (Johannes III) Lindemann. He appears in the matriculation record of Wittenberg University on 14 June 1533 with three friends from Gotha; following the death in 1546 of Luther's friend Friedrich Myconius of Gotha, Cyriac married Myconius's daughter Barbara; after various assignments in Freiberg and Meissen, Cyriac returned to Wittenberg to receive his master's degree (and to be guest at Luther's table); he spent several years as organizer and rector of the school in Schulpforte, but was forced to leave owing to local Catholic opposition; and eventually he returned to Gotha in 1549 to become corector and, after 1562, rector of the school there.[12] The proposition that Cyriac was Luther's uncle is self-evidently false. It would involve, Knaake exclaims, the passage of a whole century between the birth of Cyriac's sister and his entry into his last office! There are similar problems with the Meissen branch: the doctor is presumably Dr. Laurentius Lindemann, born 17 September 1520, whose father Caspar, physician to the Elector of Saxony and close associate of Luther's, was certainly not Luther's uncle.[13] Moreover, the repeated references to Franconia do not accord with the statements of Melanchthon and others that Luther's mother was born in Eisenach, nor with the matriculation records of other Lindemanns.[14]

It is scarcely surprising that this account should be fraught with errors—it is, after all, an eighteenth-century footnote on a seventeenth-century allusion to letters about rough notes taken from a sixteenth-century speech. Nevertheless, the relationship claimed is a very close one: Salome Beerwald's father Johann Lindemann is said to be Martin Luther's first cousin, and this agrees with Rector Schneidewein's earlier testimony to the Lindemann connection. So this evidence is not to be dismissed out of hand.

III

What case, then, can be made for the alternative tradition, that Hanna Luder was born a Ziegler? The earliest source for this tradition is the prolific controversialist Cyriac Spangenberg, pastor of Mansfeld. In his 1571 book, "15 Sermons About the Faithful Servant of Jesus Christ, Dr. Martin Luther," Spangenberg gave Luther's lineage with great confidence, but without a specific source:

I say with good grounds in the declarations and reports of reliable, honorable people that Hans Nas, Sylvius, Cochlaeus, Wicelius, and others like them who slander Luther in this way—saying that he was begotten illegitimately or by the devil and was born from a pregnant bathmaid—they lie from their throat and mouth coming and going, and against their conscience. . . . For it is certain and true, that Hans Luder, or Luther, with the knowledge and wish of his father Heine Luder and his mother Margrethe (who is by birth a Lindemann, and is buried in the high altar at Mansfeld in the Vale) united himself with Margrethe Ziegler in holy matrimony, and after regular church custom the couple were publicly betrothed at Möhra in the district or jurisdiction of Altenstein, under the Duke of Saxony, between Eisenach and Salzungen (where Burckhart Hund, and after him his son, held office), and were given to each other. And afterwards they were with each other in the county of Mansfeld when they came to Eisleben, where Hans Luder pursued his work in the mines faithfully and industriously, and through a rich smelting master, called Hans Lüttich, was so promoted that he was eventually able to enter the smelting business himself; and he lived with his Margrethe in a peaceable marriage for fifty years, and by God's blessing honorably begot children with her.[15]

It must be allowed that Knaake has excellent reasons for placing his trust in Spangenberg. Spangenberg's testimony is a deliberate attempt to adduce evidence for Luther's parentage, which implies a special concern for accuracy. Furthermore, he was ideally placed to have access to this information. Cyriac Spangenberg, youngest son of Luther's friend Johann Spangenberg, was born on 7 June 1528, at Nordhausen.[16] He matriculated at Wittenberg in 1542, already well prepared at the age of fourteen. Because of Johann Spangenberg's friendship with the faculty, Luther and Melanchthon both took special interest in the lad's studies. When he graduated in 1546, he moved immediately, at the age of eighteen, into a teaching post in the gymnasium at Eisleben. When his father died during the plague in 1550, Cyriac took over his preaching duties; in 1553 he became deacon at Mansfeld. For the next six years he worked alongside Luther's friend, Pastor Michael Cölius, who had ministered to Luther's parents on their deathbeds and then to Luther himself on his deathbed.[17] Spangenberg succeeded to the office of pastor in Mansfeld upon Cölius's death in 1559, and was appointed by the counts of Mansfeld as town and court preacher. By his personal knowledge of the Luther family, and by his close association with both Cölius and the Eisleben-Mansfeld area, Spangenberg was in an excellent position to know what he was talking about; moreover, as a student he had concentrated on sharpening his historical skills. For all that, Knaake is overconfident when he claims that Spangenberg's testimony differs in no case from otherwise established facts.[18]

Spangenberg says that Luther's grandmother, whom he calls Margrethe Lindemann, was buried in the high altar at Mansfeld. It is from this assertion that Knaake and following him both Köstlin and Boehmer, and in turn many modern biographers, all suppose that at some point the old woman moved to Mansfeld to spend her declining years in the home of Hans and Hanna Luder and died there in 1521.[19] It seems a little unlikely that an elderly country widow would leave her village and her kinsfolk and move to a strange town many miles away, even if her businessman son Hans was the most prosperous of her children. So this reconstruction is at least questionable, and the Henneberg church historian Wilhelm Germann contradicts it. Germann says that Luther's grandmother was still living at Möhra when Luther visited his relatives there in May 1521 on his return from Worms, and that she died there on 21 September 1521.[20] Unfortunately, Germann does not identify his evidence, so both the time and place of her burial must remain tentative for us.

Germann also points out two minor errors of political fact in Spangenberg's account. Spangenberg places Möhra within the administrative district of Altenstein, whereas it belonged to the Salzungen jurisdiction; and accordingly the identification of Burckhart Hund as the responsible officer is incorrect.[21] These are minor points, but they do cast doubt on Spangenberg's precision when he is dealing with events that took place many years earlier, before his own birth.

Knaake, in placing his confidence in Spangenberg, also appears to have confused two different grandmothers! In his treatment of Rector Schneidewein's announcement, he argues (as we have seen) that the maternal grandmother was a Lindemann; now he relies on Spangenberg who says that the paternal grandmother was a Lindemann. The case begins to look less plausible. Nevertheless, for several decades after Knaake wrote it was generally agreed that the Ziegler tradition had prevailed—especially when Heinrich Boehmer in 1926 established that there had indeed been a well-to-do farming family of Zieglers in the village of Möhra.[22] Since the seventeenth century many biographers had been attracted by von Seckendorff's theory that Ziegler was possibly only a trade title for some Lindemanns who were brick-makers, and that this was the source of all the confusion.[23] But Boehmer discovered that indeed the Zieglers and the Luders were two of the leading farm families in sixteenth-century Möhra, and a marriage between their clans seemed altogether plausible.[24]

IV

The solution to the puzzle began to emerge in 1934 and 1935. In a note to volume 5 of Luther's letters in the Weimar Edition (1934), Otto Clemen partially reconstructed the genealogical record of the Lindemann family.[25] Then in 1935 Eberhard Matthes completed the reconstruction of the family tree, and in

the process proved that Spangenberg was wrong.[26] Margarethe
Luder was born Margarethe Lindemann, daughter of Johann (I)
Lindemann, burgher in Eisenach. Not only was Rector Schneidewein predictably correct, but Pastor Beerwald was also vindi-
cated in his main assertions. The reported version of his remarks
certainly confused the generations of his wife's second cousins,
but his father-in-law was indeed Luther's first cousin, and Luther
did in fact have three maternal uncles, one in Eisleben, one in
Eisenach, and one in Neustadt.

The sources of this reconstruction were many. Most of the
official archives of Eisenach itself were destroyed by fire in
1636, so Matthes examined the letters and table talk of Luther
himself; a letter of Melanchthon's in which he identifies Philipp
Lindemann (Salome Beerwald's brother) as "a relative of
Luther's"; university records at Leipzig, Wittenberg, Frankfurt,
and Bologna; school records at Gotha and Schweinfurt; city
archives and assessors' book at Gotha; parish records and tomb-
stones from Leipzig, Gotha, and Rodewisch; histories of Eisenach,
Mansfeld, and Schneeberg; personal memorials; and a manuscript (Stadtbibliothek, Leipzig) by Joh[ann] Jacob Vogel,
"Florilegium Genealogicum Lipsiense," which includes an invaluable "Genealogia Lindemanniana." The resulting family tree,
as Matthes culled it from these records, is summarized in the
accompanying table on pp. 30–31.

The key pieces of additional evidence by which Matthes con-
clusively links Luther's mother to the Lindemann family are
four in number. One is a letter of 4 January 1526 from Stephan
Roth to his friend Theodor Lindemann, schoolmaster and later
mayor of Dresden. Roth's closing messages say in part: "Give
my greeting . . . also to your relative M. Luther, who when he
was a baccalaureus at Erfurt once gave me warm hospitality in
the George Burse for several days. . . ."[27] The second is a letter
from Melanchthon to Georg Karg in Ansbach on 27 October
1555, commending Philipp Lindemann who had just graduated
from Wittenberg:

Hereby I commend to you Philipp Lindemann, a cognate relative of
Luther's, outstandingly learned in Latin and Greek, church teaching,

philosophy, and natural ethics. . . . I so commend him that, to the extent you would wish to assist a son of my own, so you will assist him, whom for his virtues I love as a son.[28]

The third is an epigram of 8 August 1584, composed by Ludwig Helmbold, superintendent of Mühlhausen, and dedicated to his recently deceased friend, Cyriac Lindemann:

Begotten of an Eisenach father, Gotha was his country,
And he was linked by blood with Luther's parents.
A tailor was his father, the tailor's son
Progressed to noble skills: so God teaches one to go.[29]

The fourth piece of decisive evidence also concerns Cyriac Lindemann, this time a memorial oration given in his honor in 1592 by Johann Dinckel, general superintendent at Coburg:

Least of all should we omit to mention, I think, that he was linked by blood with that great German prophet Luther since Luther's mother was born of the family of the Lindemanns, and was sister of Cyriac Lindemann's grandfather, so that she is rightly called his great-aunt. Hence it appears that this Mr. Lindemann was related to the divine Luther in the third degree of consanguinity by an indirect line, and while Luther was still alive he received many kindnesses from him, as he affirmed in letters he wrote to Theodor Lindemann, councillor at Dresden.[30]

Why, then, did Spangenberg give incorrect information? We shall return in the next chapter to examine Spangenberg's worthy motive in adducing this detail. As a matter of fact, he also showed elsewhere that his knowledge of the Lindemann family was incomplete,[31] but in Mansfeld he ought to have been in an ideal position to know the truth about Luther's parents. Heinrich Bornkamm has already conjectured that Spangenberg's information was correct, but that he simply reversed the generations: Luther's mother was a Lindemann, his grandmother a Ziegler.[32] Is it possible that the tomb in the church at Lower Mansfeld was the source of the confusion? It is unlikely that Spangenberg could have been wrong about the very existence of such a burial place in his own parish church. But on the face of it, it is more likely that Luther's mother was buried there than his grandmother. However, Spangenberg's source for the Ziegler tradition remains for now a matter of conjecture. What is beyond doubt is that Margarethe Luder was a daughter of the well-established Eisenach family Lindemann.

LUTHER'S LINDEMANN COUSINS
(after Eberhard Matthes, "Luthers mütterliche Abstammung," p. 214)

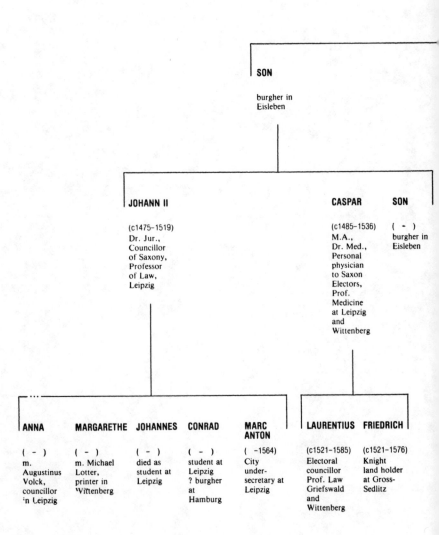

SON

burgher in
Eisleben

JOHANN II

(c1475–1519)
Dr. Jur.,
Councillor
of Saxony,
Professor
of Law,
Leipzig

CASPAR

(c1485–1536)
M.A.,
Dr. Med.,
Personal
physician
to Saxon
Electors,
Prof.
Medicine
at Leipzig
and
Wittenberg

SON

(-)
burgher in
Eisleben

ANNA

(-)
m.
Augustinus
Volck,
councillor
in Leipzig

MARGARETHE

(-)
m. Michael
Lotter,
printer in
Wittenberg

JOHANNES

(-)
died as
student at
Leipzig

CONRAD

(-)
student at
Leipzig
? burgher
at
Hamburg

**MARC
ANTON**

(–1564)
City
under-
secretary at
Leipzig

LAURENTIUS

(c1521–1585)
Electoral
councillor
Prof. Law
Griefswald
and
Wittenberg

FRIEDRICH

(c1521–1576)
Knight
land holder
at Gross-
Sedlitz

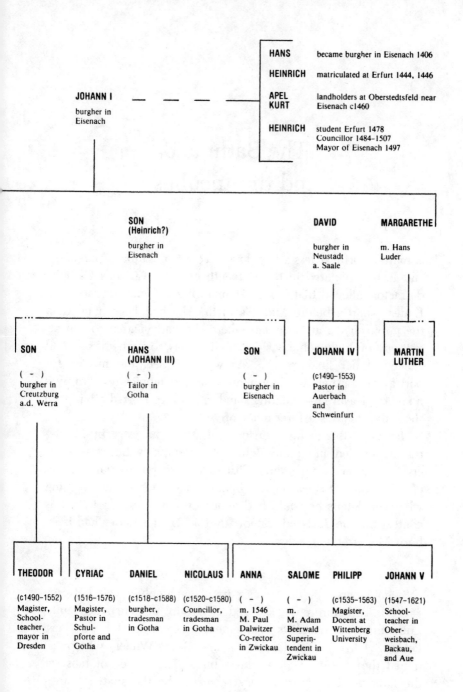

JOHANN I
burgher in
Eisenach

HANS became burgher in Eisenach 1406

HEINRICH matriculated at Erfurt 1444, 1446

APEL
KURT landholders at Oberstedtsfeld near
Eisenach c1460

HEINRICH student Erfurt 1478
Councillor 1484–1507
Mayor of Eisenach 1497

SON
(Heinrich?)
burgher in
Eisenach

DAVID
burgher in
Neustadt
a. Saale

MARGARETHE
m. Hans
Luder

SON
(–)
burgher in
Creutzburg
a.d. Werra

HANS
(JOHANN III)
(–)
Tailor in
Gotha

SON
(–)
burgher in
Eisenach

JOHANN IV
(c1490–1553)
Pastor in
Auerbach
and
Schweinfurt

MARTIN
LUTHER

THEODOR
(c1490–1552)
Magister,
School-
teacher,
mayor in
Dresden

CYRIAC
(1516–1576)
Magister,
Pastor in
Schul-
pforte and
Gotha

DANIEL
(c1518–c1588)
burgher,
tradesman
in Gotha

NICOLAUS
(c1520–c1580)
Councillor,
tradesman
in Gotha

ANNA
(–)
m. 1546
M. Paul
Dalwitzer
Co-rector
in Zwickau

SALOME
(–)
m.
M. Adam
Beerwald
Superin-
tendent in
Zwickau

PHILIPP
(c1535–1563)
Magister,
Docent at
Wittenberg
University

JOHANN V
(1547–1621)
School-
teacher in
Ober-
weisbach,
Backau,
and Aue

3

The Bathmaid
and the Incubus

A more colorful if less scrupulous account of Luther's parentage
and birth circulated in the sixteenth century. Luther's Catholic
detractors alleged that before Hanna's hurried marriage to Hans
Luder (shortly before Martin's birth) she had been a maid in
the public baths at Eisleben, where she had yielded to the at-
tentions of a demonic visitor, an incubus, by whom she had
conceived her firstborn son. As we shall see, the motive for
portraying Luther as illegitimately and demonically born was
no mere pleasure in titillating slander, but a concerted attempt to
show that he was a forerunner of Antichrist.

Naturally, this malign version of Luther's ancestry by his detractors evoked an equally deliberate attempt by Lutheran writers to counteract such slurs with their own reverential account
of his origins. This was Cyriac Spangenberg's motive in amassing
whatever details he could find about Luther's birth; it is in this
context that he declared confidently that Hanna Luder had been
born Margarethe Ziegler.

I

Spangenberg's account was part of a pamphlet war between
various Lutheran eulogists and a group of outspoken anti-
Lutheran propagandists (Spangenberg names Johann Nas,
Petrus Sylvius, Johann Cochlaeus, and Georg Witzel) who questioned the legitimacy of Luther's birth. The source of most of
the later versions of the story seems to be the spate of anti-

Luther pamphlets written by one of the stranger minor characters of the Catholic opposition, the hypochondriacal Petrus Sylvius.[1] Sylvius was born in Forsta about 1470, matriculated at Leipzig in 1491 as "Petrus Penick von Forst," and progressed to baccalaureus in 1501 and to magister in 1508. In spite of the rich benefices and school positions thus made available to him, he entered the Dominican cloister at Leipzig as a postulant—"in my stupidity and imprudence," he said later. He was totally unfit for the rigors of the cloistered life: his memories of his year's postulancy were of repeated illness, a horrible unvarying diet of inedible eggs, and a laxity in the face of the observance which made it obvious to everyone that he was unsuitable. He ignored his superiors' advice and was professed, but three years of illnesses and torpor and the endless choir offices and hunger later drove him from his purpose, and he sought and obtained freedom from his vows and became a secular priest instead.

It was on his journey to Rome in 1514 to obtain dispensation from Leo X that Sylvius also visited the shrine of Mary of Loreto, and here the key event took place—a marvelous heavenly illumination which awoke in him a special capacity for distinguishing between Christian truth and heretical falsehood. The result was to be an obsessive outpouring of anti-Lutheran tracts, in which *inter alia* the story of Luther's birth from the devil and a bathmaid was first published.

Sylvius claimed later to be the very first person to write against Luther. Even before the Leipzig Disputation he had penned a tractate against the Lutheran theses and predicted Luther's stand against the decretals and councils, but he could not afford to have the book published. This seems to have been his frustration for several years. By the early 1520s he had composed at least twenty-five German tracts, but stable employment eluded him, and thus the wherewithal to have them printed. In 1524 he was preacher at Kronschwitz, and at the end of that year became pastor of Weida, only to be forced out in a few weeks by the Lutheran burghers. He found a post at Lohma near Schmollen, was pressed by the burghers to celebrate the German mass and give communion in both kinds, and engaged in public disputation on the issue with Wenceslaus Link, but was again forced out, this time by the Peasants' War. He fled to Dresden, where at last he began to have his .tractates published—"at my own expense, as much as I was able to afford." A few booklets appeared at Leipzig and Dresden, often numbered but not in the order in which they were written; after Duke George at last found a chaplaincy for Sylvius at Rochlitz in 1528, remaining numbers in the series were published, twenty-eight of them by 1534.

It is in booklets 15 and 28 that the story of Luther's mother first appears. In its fullest form in *The Last Two Booklets* . . . (the version from which the later tradition flows) Sylvius's account reads:

First I say, with divine truth, that Luther is, above all heretics and arch-heretics who have been since the beginning of the faith, not only the most utterly unchristian, most seductive and most damnable heretic, but he is also in truth really a possessed, devilish man, a pipe and trumpet of the evil spirits, who through him play whatever tune they like in the world. Above all he is really and truly a most outstanding and special forerunner of the Antichrist himself. . . . He had a birth equal to the real Antichrist, for he was begotten and born through action of the evil spirit. . . .

For according to the trustworthy account of an upright God-fearing woman, as she heard it from Luther's mother herself, before she bore Luther his mother was a secret playmate, of which she boasted, because she served in the bath house at Eisleben as one who was still a maiden. So one can readily judge Luther's origin. She had boasted, namely, how at night, through closed doors, a handsome young man in red clothing had come to her often before Shrovetide and said many uncommonly strange words to her in a hoarse voice, and would neither eat nor drink, he would not marry her nor make foolish promises to do so before her company, but promised that he would have her married after Easter to a wealthy businessman, and she should confess it to no-one or else he would not come to her anymore. And so it happened that after Easter for her reward and hope a businessman named Luder pressed her to marry him, and sometime about Pentecost they held their wedding, and not so very long afterwards Martin Luther was born in Eisleben just before St. Martin's day (as he himself writes), was baptized and named Martin. I have thoroughly argued and described this in Booklet 15, but I omitted there to mention only one thing—that I had written these things down just as I received them at the time from the very person who had herself heard them from Luther's mother, for she was companion to Luther's mother with whom she shared a house at the time, and often heard such things, and far more than I can describe here. . . .

From these few words and accounts written here, any reasonable person can discover that Luther was begotten long before the marriage by an incarnate evil spirit in human form, called an Incubus, and thus was begotten according to the form of the true Antichrist through action of the evil fiend. And without any doubt the same evil spirit was soon implanted in his heart in the womb, so that he was born and raised to no other purpose than only to prepare all error, discord, uproar, war, bloodshed, corruption, and damnation for Christendom. So too in his childhood he always had such strange and wild manners and tastes that it was said of him that he upset many people and they used to say, "No good will come of that child." And especially his mother, who knew somewhat more of his doings, always grieved greatly, and at length (as I have heard from many people even in the Electoral territory) wretchedly deplored and bemoaned his new teaching, and uttered some frightening words, namely that it would rue her forever that she had not killed the child in the cradle, and many similar things which for the sake of brevity I leave aside here. But that I heard all these things that I have described here about Luther's origin from a well-informed person, as did many other brave men and highly intelligent lords and doctors, and that I have not made them up myself, I have protested in my fifteenth booklet, printed at another time. . . .[2]

The protestation referred to in booklet 15, accompanying the same story, declares:

But that I have not made up these doings myself, but that they were passed on by a well-informed person often and (as I first heard it) a long time ago, as early as the Leipzig Disputation, I can maintain before God with a sure conscience, and if I were questioned further by constituted authority, I can identify the woman who first told me about it, and those who were with me in this woman's presence and heard all these things with me from her own mouth.[3]

The story was certainly current in Leipzig circles even before Sylvius saw booklets 15 and 28 through the press. Those others of Luther's opponents who mention it, however, obviously take it with less than the earnest conviction accorded it by the discerning Sylvius. Georg Witzel, in an open letter written to Justus Jonas in 1532 but published in 1535 as part of his *Expostulation Concerning the Theft of a Private Letter*, makes a testy but fleeting reference: "But if it were to become a public issue, I could mention the murder committed by your Luther's father, or speak as others do about his mother's incubus (even if finally nothing is known for certain about this) . . . but I am unwilling to imitate your defamatory habits. . . ."[4] (In a second edition, two years later, the slander against Luther's father is repeated, but interestingly the reference to his mother has been dropped.[5]) About the same time, Abbot Paul Bachmann (Amnicola) is similarly tentative in his booklet, *A Punch in the Mouth for the Lutheran Lying Wide-gaping Throats* . . . (1534): "As to what sort of father Luther had, then I might write or say (as others declare) that the devil was his father! But I let it rest at that and do not reproach you with it."[6] The earliest reference to the story from the pen of Johann Cochlaeus, the most formidable of these gainsayers, appears in the 1533 German version of his *Defense of Duke George* (which Luther momentarily supposed was the Duke's own production). Cochlaeus calls Luther "a lousy renegade monk and nun's-fanny who owns neither land nor people, an ignoble changeling born of a bathmaid, as they say. . . ."[7]

Though Luther never mentioned Sylvius, he was certainly aware that Cochlaeus had slandered his parentage. At table that same year, during a conversation about Cochlaeus, Luther said: "He calls me a changeling brat and also a bathmaid's son, two things which cannot co-exist in the same individual; because one, the changeling, is altered by Satan and different from a real man, but the other is a natural human son."[8] Although this may sound almost tongue-in-cheek, it was no joke to Luther: five years later he again quoted Cochlaeus word for word at table;[9] and in 1543, after ten years, Luther bitterly resurrected the slander in *On the Jews and Their Lies*:

These are the kinds of lies that the devil resorts to if he can't do the teaching any harm—he turns against the person, he lies, slanders, curses and raves against him. Just as the papist Beelzebub did to me when he could not withstand my gospel: he wrote that I had a devil, that I was a changeling, my dear mother a whore and a bathmaid.[10]

The currency of the story in ducal Saxony is also reflected in the report that Pietro Paulo Vergerio, the papal legate in Germany, sent to Rome from Dresden after his mismatched breakfast meeting with Luther in November 1535. After describing the gruffness of Luther's speech, his startling eyes, and his passionate manner, Vergerio adds, "from what I know of his birth and all of his past life from persons who were his intimate friends at the time he became a brother, I am almost ready to believe that he does have some kind of demon."[11] Hieronymus Aleander, Luther's chief prosecutor at Worms, took pains to copy and circulate Vergerio's account.

But it is Cochlaeus, after Luther's death, who gives the story its widest currency. In the preface to his 1549 *Commentaria . . . de actis et scriptis Martini Lutheri,* he cleverly and equivocally reports:

There are those who affirm that Luther was begotten by an unclean spirit under the appearance of an incubus. They adduce a witness of this fact, a certain godly old woman who lives in Leipzig, who knew Luther's mother when she was a maid in the public bath at Eisleben, and who heard about a young man, whom she thinks was an incubus, by whom Luther's mother was impregnated before she had known her husband, Johann Luder. We ourselves do not affix our trust to this affirmation, even though it has been relayed in writing. . . .[12]

Though Cochlaeus withholds his own sanction in this particular as in others, he succeeded in influencing much of the later Catholic historiography about Luther (as Adolf Herte has documented),[13] and the story is repeated down into the nineteenth century.

In the transmission of Cochlaeus's account, even Erasmus is drawn in as an unwitting deponent. Gabriel Dupréau (Prateolus) was the compiler of a massive 1569 encyclopedia of heresies and heretics "from the beginning of the world to our own times." Lavish space was devoted to all the varieties of "Lutheranism"— that is, the Protestant sects, already so fragmented—and above all, to the heresiarch Luther himself. Discussing one of Luther's books, Prateolus says:

About the author there is certainly no shortage of evidence (in no way abhorrent to truth) that this and his other works were dictated to him not by a human spirit, nor yet divine, but by a diabolical spirit, just as also Montanus by the spirit Pythonicus, or Mahomet by the spirit Gabriel, the devil transforming himself into an angel of light. For there are those who have written that Luther was begotten by an incubus which forced itself on his mother when she was a serving maid at a public bath; but I do not know who the source was. Yet in the account of his life collected from the sources by the worthy lord Cochlaeus it is recorded that certain people had attested to it in letters. But the source may perhaps be that Leipzig matron to whom his mother was very well known. It is not inconsistent with truth that Erasmus alludes to this story. After Luther had reproached him for perpetrating certain obscene expressions that Erasmus had in fact never written in that form, Erasmus said in rebuttal of this public aspersion of foulness: "It is surely surprising that he added to his impious and blasphemous accusation nothing about the incubi who are said to go into women. Such an aspersion against a maligned enemy would have been just as false, except that (even from a distance, like a smell) it would have betrayed by its baseness a man more raving than Orestes, and by its Satanic cursing a man most wantonly bitter; and this may restrain his filthy speech."[14]

In this contrived way, even the great humanist is forced to attest to Luther's demonic origins.

As an instance of the possibilities of elaboration offered by such a fable, we may note the dissenting contribution of Dr. Johann Wier.[15] Wier (or Weier, Weyer, Vierus) was born in 1515 at Grave in Nordbrabant, which was then a German state. As a teenager, he studied for some time with Cornelius Agrippa in Antwerp. He began the study of medicine at Paris in 1534 and continued at Orléans, graduating in 1537. By 1545 he was city physician at Arnhem, from 1550 onwards he was personal physician to Duke Wilhelm III of Jühlich-Cleve-Berg, and he soon established a reputation as one of Europe's outstanding medical minds. His several volumes of *Observationes medicae* became a standard reference, especially for the treatment of rare and exotic diseases. But Wier is also outstanding for another reason. In an age when the horrible and oppressive obsession with witchcraft and demonism was ever more widespread, he was one of the earliest and most clearsighted of those who attacked the inhumanity of the legal process against witches. His treatise *On the Illusions of Demons* went through several expanding editions in the 1560s and 1570s. It exposed the gullibility and superstition of those who could believe in the power of such figments. There is no reference to Luther's birth in the 1562 Latin first edition. In the 1566 German edition, Wier gives a list of people said to be of supernatural conception, and after mentioning Hector, Achilles, Aeneas, Hercules, and Plato, adds cautiously:

I have also read in a French book written by a theologian how Luther was born from the intercourse of an obscene devil and a woman. But I should warn such learned people about this—by their leave, of course, since I am only a mere physician or doctor—that they ought not presume to attack Luther's teaching with such fabrication, but only with the salutary Word of God. . . .[16]

In order to illustrate that this advice was necessary, in the much longer 1568 Latin edition Wier added a whole chapter on Luther's alleged demonic origin.[17] Most of the chapter is devoted to retailing a fable he had heard from a bishop at a renowned university: how the devil in the form of a gem merchant had visited Wittenberg, and under the pretext of offering large sums for the Wittenbergers' precious stones had seduced one of the daughters of the town. Her illegitimate child had been unnaturally brilliant at school, had become a monk, but after visiting Rome had attacked the pope and the cardinals, and had led astray not only many common people but even some of the learned. Wier then repeats the short form of the older story from his French source, whom he now identifies as the Paris Franciscan Simon Fontaine, whose *Histoire catholique de nostre temps* (1558) drew in turn on Cochlaeus's *Commentaria*.[18] At the end, Wier again calls these stories "figments" and adds Luther's own familiar brief account of his birth date and parentage.

Wier's *caveat* generally went unheeded. For our purposes the significant transmitter of the bathmaid tradition is the fierce controversialist Johann Nas; for it was against Nas that Cyriac Spangenberg was writing when he identified Hanna Luder as a Ziegler by birth.

Nas, later bishop of Brixen, was born 19 March 1534, in Eltmann, East Franconia.[19] He became a Franciscan monk at Munich, was ordained a priest in 1557 at Freising, and in 1559 was sent by his order to the University of Ingolstadt, where the trenchant anti-Lutheran tradition of Johann Eck was still flourishing. Here Nas learned the arts of theological polemic from the masters of the trade, and the chief result was a series of six *Hundreds*, beginning in 1567. Each volume contained exactly one hundred polemical arguments, in which Nas capitalized on the factionalism and infighting of his Protestant targets, notably Brenz, Flacius, Manlius, Musculus, Lukas Osiander, and Hessius; in the fifth *Hundred* his special target was Cyriac Spangenberg.[20]

Like Cochlaeus, Nas's great skill as a controversialist was that he knew his subject matter intimately, including the most recent publications of his opponents. He had taken the trouble to find and read all of Petrus Sylvius's anti-Lutheran tracts, and quoted the story of Luther's birth from them at length and almost verbatim. He knew Cochlaeus's writings, including the relevant passage from the preface to the *Commentaria*. He even knew Luther's own reaction to the story from Aurifaber's collection of the *Table Talk*: to Luther's contention that a changeling and a bathmaid's son could not coexist in one man, Nas scornfully rejoined "Why not?" He had read Melanchthon's biographical introduction to Luther's writings. He knew the series of biographical sermons preached about Luther by Mathesius and by Spangenberg; and it was these series which were the immediate occasion of his 1570 *Quinta Centuria*.[21] Nas's motive in retelling the story in all Sylvius's murky detail was a refutation of the claim he found in the reverent accounts of Mathesius and Spangenberg, the claim that Luther was not only honorably and legitimately born, but that signs of divine favor marked him out in advance as a special messenger of God, "justifying," as Nas said disdainfully, "an equation with John the Baptist, Jeremiah, and others who were wonderfully born." Whereas Spangenberg identified Luther with Elijah, the divine forerunner of the end, Nas reverted to Sylvius's old claim that Luther was indeed a forerunner, a harbinger of the end, but the prophesied forerunner of the Antichrist himself.

Cyriac Spangenberg's sermons, which finally numbered fifteen, were published in parts in the early 1560s. Nas treated their claims for an honorable birth for Luther very scornfully. For this reason, Spangenberg included in the complete 1571 edition of all fifteen sermons a list of names and places and circumstances all designed to confirm his version of the facts and to silence Nas's slanders. It was in this deposition, offered "with good grounds in the declarations and reports of reliable, honorable people," that the name "Ziegler" is first mentioned—incorrectly—as Margarethe Luder's family name.

II

A besetting difficulty of all Luther biography is that the earliest sources, whether friendly or hostile, are anything but dispassionate. Not only are they fiercely partisan and mutually pejorative, written in an age which had perfected the art of vituperation, but they often had specific ideological axes to grind.

In retrospect, we can see the ways in which sixteenth-century religious polemics contributed to the development of modern European historiography: the desire for "evidence" in support of controverted claims; the attempt to chronicle bitterly opposed interpretations of the direction of history or of the identity of the true church; above all, the systematic collection of documents to support massive ventures in history and propaganda. (Flacius Illyricus's collecting of books and manuscripts, in preparation for the Lutheran world-history, *The Magdeburg Centuries,* is one of the great bibliographic feats, and created the basic collections of several major European libraries.) In the early years, however, we would look in vain for a commitment to objectivity. Rather the opposite is true. In the case of Luther's origins, for example, we discover both sides speciously pointing to their "sources" as they proceed with little subtlety to match Luther with an existing religious image, the eschatalogical figure of the forerunner.[22]

Of course, there were two sorts of forerunner in popular expectation: the Elijah figure who would signal the approach of the second coming, and the malevolent figure of Antichrist who would mark the imminent onset of the great tribulation. Both were familiar images from the age-old tradition of advent sermons on the signs of the end. Generation after generation of preachers had passed on graphic details—now interpreted literally, now figuratively—about the circumstances of Antichrist's birth, and the state of the world at his rising.[23] The time before the coming of Antichrist would be a time of falling away: a secession of peoples from the Roman Empire, of various churches from the Roman obedience, and of some Christians from the catholic faith. St. John Damascene was quoted as authority for believing that "Antichrist would be born of the condemned intercourse of bastardy." While he was still in the womb of his whorish mother, this Antichrist would be filled with the spirit of the devil: a malign spirit would descend on his mother's womb, and by its power and operation the child would be brought forth, and nourished. The elements of the bathmaid story lay ready at hand.

But there was more. This forerunner would be called "the son of perdition" because he would actively solicit the perdition of others, and would conquer the wise of the world by false arguments and false exposition of scripture. His ministers would make merry and take wives. Whereas Christ was humble, chaste, and poor, the Antichrist would be proud, lustful, and rich. In his train, many false preachers and teachers would arise, tricksters in deceit, who would seduce many by the Antichrist's newfangled doctrines and disturb the faithful. These heretics would confess their faith in words, but destroy it by their way of life and corrupt it by their habits; they would contradict the truth of the church and work against its mandates.

All these motifs were common coin in the religious culture on the eve of the Reformation, and it was a relatively simple task for Catholic polemicists to sound these familiar chords in describing Luther. His assault on papal power, refusal to recant heresy, and defiance of the emperor, his abandoning monastic vows, his marriage to a nun, his haughtiness in dispute, the charismatic appeal of his presence, his language, his eyes—all these could be portrayed with occult overtones of the Antichrist, the heresiarch, the forerunner of the final great schism. It was simple and effective propaganda to include the manner of Luther's birth, and with it the person of his mother, in this infernal image.

But the very same preaching tradition contained themes that Luther's eulogists could use in rebuttal. The advent tradition foretold that in the time of Antichrist God would send Enoch and Elijah to strengthen the faithful remnant and prophesy Christ's kingdom. Luther, who had denounced the pope as Antichrist, was early seen by his own followers as a special messenger from God. In his lifetime, Luther resisted attempts to find astrological proof of his singularity,[24] though he was not averse to seeing himself, in his God-given calling, as a prophet.[25] Others were less reticent. Various members of Luther's circle—Melanchthon, Myconius, Mathesius, perhaps even Luther himself—took with great seriousness certain prophecies made by the elderly Franciscan visionary Johann Hilten (ca. 1425–1500) in his commentaries on Daniel, notably that a potent reformer would appear in 1516.[26] Melanchthon even referred to these predictions in the *Apology* to the Augsburg Confession, thus making public claim in the highest councils of the empire to the divine origins of Luther's mission.[27] But it was after Luther's death that his identification as a forerunner became most explicit among his disciples.

When Pastor Michael Cölius preached the funeral sermon for Martin Luther on 19 February 1546 in Eisleben, he first dismissed the slanders, already widespread, about Luther's birth:

Yet this city of Eisleben and the whole territory of Mansfeld knows even so that he was born in wedlock from honorable, godly parents right here in Eisleben, and baptized as a Christian, and after six months his parents took him with them to Mansfeld, where they then spent the greatest part of their life, and there also ended this life, and both father and mother, as the dear man of God himself, in my own hands, with heartfelt confession of their faith and calling on the name of God, fell asleep in the Lord, in God's eternal grace.[28]

Having attested the honor of the family and the firmness of their faith, Cölius then proceeded to compare Luther's appearance to Elijah, and Jeremiah, and John the Baptist in their own times. In Wittenberg, three days later, Dr. Johann Bugenhagen went even further in his memorial address of 22 February 1546: "He was without any doubt the angel who is described in Revelation 14, who 'flies through the heaven and has an eternal gospel to proclaim to those on earth. . . .' "[29] Then Bugenhagen went on to expound Revelation 14's visions of apocalypse and judgment in terms of Luther's life and ministry. Thereafter, the honorable, legitimate, and godly nature of Luther's birth, and the special marks of divine favor upon his prophetic mission as forerunner, become standard features of the hagiographical tradition in Lutheranism.

III

Luther's mother thus appears in both versions of his more-than-ordinary-birth: in one as an upright, chaste, and godly wife; in the other as a bathmaid, a whore, a playmate, a devil's trull. But sadly, in neither does she appear in her own right; she is introduced, for the most part anonymously, simply as a pawn in a wider ideological game about her illustrious son. Since for their purposes she was only a means to an end, the controversialists tended to place her in one or other of the roles—saint or whore—which men have customarily assigned to women. What is lost in the process is the more complex human contribution she actually made to Luther's development.

4

Martin Among
His Mother's People

Margarethe Luder was born Margarethe Lindemann, not Margarethe Ziegler. It is not her name, however, that is important, but rather her family background. If she had been a Ziegler, as Spangenberg claimed, then her social background would have been markedly different from what it was in fact—and with it, perhaps, her husband's fortunes and her son's career.

For the Zieglers and the Lindemanns were very different sorts of families. The Zieglers were a farm family in the village of Möhra—not cottagers from the landless ranks of poor peasant laborers, but well-to-do landholders enjoying inherited tax advantages. Heinrich Boehmer discovered from local archives that in 1536, among the quitrent inhabitants of Möhra, there were five households each in the four biggest families—Kehr, Luder, Mentzer, and Ziegler—with stock and property assessed respectively at 841, 1008, 1140, and 1182 gulden.[1] In other words, the Zieglers were the most comfortable of these relatively prosperous peasants, and the leading villager was Hans Ziegler, who alone valued his property at 600 gulden and his herd at 40 gulden. The Zieglers and the Luders, in short, were socially very similar families.

The Lindemanns, however, were a family of a very different sort. They were a well-established and respected family of Eisenach burghers: one Hans Lindemann was recorded as a citizen of Eisenach in 1406, and a Heinrich Lindemann matriculated at Erfurt in 1444 and 1445. Another Heinrich Lindemann, also an Erfurt graduate, was a city councillor from 1484 to 1507 (together with Heinrich Schalbe) and mayor in 1497.[2]

In Luther's own generation and the two that followed, the Lindemanns produced a remarkable array of prominent, highly educated, professional people. Among Luther's first cousins, for example, was Johann (II) Lindemann of Eisleben (1475–1519), doctor of civil and canon law of the University of Leipzig in 1514, and councillor of ducal Saxony.[3] Johann's brother was Caspar Lindemann (1485–1536), who studied at Leipzig, Frankfurt an der Oder, and Bologna, and graduated as both master of arts and doctor of medicine. He became professor of medicine at Leipzig and also personal physician to both Frederick the Wise and John of Saxony. In this capacity he had occasion also to treat Luther himself. In 1532 he was called to the chair of medicine at Wittenberg, which he held until his death four years later.[4] Luther's maternal cousins and their children included two pastors, two lawyers, a physician, two schoolmasters, a university docent, and three public officials; among their qualifications, three attained the degree of doctor, three the degree of magister, two were ducal councillors, and three were mayors of their respective cities. The Lindemanns were a highly distinguished family.

I

The fact that Hanna Luder was not a Ziegler but a Lindemann thus strikingly changes our picture of the dynamics within the Luder household, both socially and psychologically. Rather than a marriage between two rural villagers who then had to struggle in hardship to make their way in the alien mining district of Mansfeld, we find that Hans Luder (with characteristic resourcefulness) made an excellent marriage into a prominent family of the nearby market town of Eisenach. Whether there was any feeling among Margarethe's patrician kinsfolk that she had married below her status we cannot tell; we do know that her circle of respected relatives and acquaintances soon gave a warm reception to her son as a schoolboy. Since Eisenach's economic prosperity was somewhat in decline, there was probably no great barrier to social mobility.

Now and then a biographer has mentioned this disparity in social class between Hans and Hanna Luder. H. E. Jacobs notes Melanchthon's report that Hanna came "from an ancient and honorable family of Eisenach";[5] B. K. Kuiper says, "She was of the burgher class, and therefore of a somewhat higher social level than Luther's father";[6] and T. M. Lindsay adds, "Hans Luther had married above his rank."[7] But in the confusion over who she was, the fact has been generally ignored and, where noted, its significance overlooked.

The Lindemann connection had important consequences for both the material and cultural direction of Hanna's own household. When the Luder family moved to Eisleben—an event that usually passes unexplained—they were not, in fact, "so far away from kith and kin."[8] Their choice of Eisleben was apparently prompted by the fact that Hanna's oldest brother, the father of Johann (II) and Caspar Lindemann, was already a burgher of that town. The rapidity of Hans Luder's rise in the Eisleben-Mansfeld district—the fact that Hans Lüttich was prepared to capitalize his venture into the smelting business and that he so soon became a member of the Mansfeld civic "committee of four"—is readily explained by the combination of his native energy and the established status of his wife's relations.

Hans Luder's ambitions for his oldest son—that he should make "an honorable and wealthy marriage" and enter the law[9]—also appear in a new light when seen in the context of the Lindemann family, where (as we have seen) the normal expectation of sons in Martin's generation was that they should enter one of the learned professions and become men of influence. In fact, we have Melanchthon's specific assertion that the Lindemanns in Eisenach urged this very course for young Martin: "On the advice of his kinsfolk, who believed that cleverness and eloquence as great as his should be brought out into the open and into public affairs, he began the study of law."[10]

But it was in the earlier years of Martin's education that the influence of Hanna's family background was specially significant. Again we have Melanchthon's testimony to the earliest stratum of his schooling:

When he was old enough to be taught, his parents accustomed the boy Martin, by diligent instruction at home, to the knowledge and fear of God and to the duties of the other virtues; and as is usual with honorable people, they took care that he should learn to read.[11]

At a time when literacy was still the prerogative of "people of honor," the Luders personally took care that their son, like his kinsfolk, should enjoy this access to power and status. Given the fact that (until the eighteenth century) there was no school in Hans's village of Möhra,[12] and that the Lindemanns were a highly educated family, we may conjecture that Hanna was the more literate of Martin's parents and exercised the greater influence on his verbal skills, both before and after he learned to read. This is a formative influence of no little weight upon a mind of such verbal genius. The first years of life are all-important for acquiring language skills; as Bruner says, a child's progress in language is "massively dependent upon the interaction of the mother . . . and the child. Mothers *teach* their children to speak, however willing the children may be."[13] Erikson says that "nobody could speak and sing as Luther later did if his mother's voice had not sung to him of some heaven."[14] We should go further: Martin Luther was one of the century's great masters of language. His mass appeal and abiding influence rested in no small measure on his verbal power, his unmatched instinct for word and image. There is no clearer testimony to Hanna's maternal influence upon him.

When he was still young enough to be carried, Martin went to the local grammar school, and later spent a year in the Latin school at Magdeburg. But it was in the critical years of his adolescence that the Lindemann family was most directly influential. In 1497—the year in which his uncle Heinrich was mayor —Martin was sent to Eisenach to school and spent the years from the age of thirteen until his matriculation at seventeen in the care of his mother's relatives. Melanchthon says explicitly that "the reason he was sent to Eisenach was that his mother had been born there of an old and respected family,"[15] and Luther himself declares in 1520 that "almost all my kinsfolk are at Eisenach" and that there "one would call Luther's son 'nephew,' another 'uncle,' another 'maternal cousin' (I have many of them there)."[16]

Reminiscing later about his school days in Eisenach, Luther says that he begged his bread from door to door;[17] but this was not the fruit of penury, but of custom. Tradition dictated that a schoolboy should "sing for his supper" in the streets as a waif, a

Partekenhengst. Yet out of this detail the biographers of the following century fabricated a romantic legend about Martin's Eisenach school days that has almost occluded the real significance of those years in the circle of his mother's family.

This poignant legend portrays a poor schoolboy begging his bread from door to door because his humble relations could not provide for him, until a wealthy widow, hearing him sing beautifully in church, took pity on him and provided him with board. From the end of the seventeenth century onward, the elaborated form of the legend identified this pious widow as Ursula Cotta, née Schalbe, widow of Kurt Cotta. From her, Luther was said to have gained entree into a circle of spiritually fervent patricians, affording him contact with Pastor Johann Braun, Vicar of St. Mary's, and the Franciscans from the retreat house at the foot of the Wartburg.

This story must now be revised in light of what we know about Martin's Eisenach relatives and also in light of what we know about Ursula Cotta. For the received tradition about her is quite wrong. In 1964 Martin Kessler investigated the genealogy of Ursula Cotta and outlined the stages by which this erroneous tradition evolved.[18]

Luther himself had referred to the burgher with whom he lodged, and whose son he guided to school, as "Heinrich," and elsewhere as "my host Heinrich Schalbe," pious devotee of the Eisenach Minorites.[19] An undated extract from Aurifaber's collection of the *Table Talk* also refers to an unidentified "hostess" from Luther's Eisenach school days from whom he heard the dictum, "There is no dearer thing on earth than a woman's love, if it fall to your lot."[20] Kessler showed how these references were conflated with the evolving legend. First, Ratzeberger (1558) identifies Luther's Eisenach host as "Cuntz Kotten." Mathesius (1562) is the source of the story about the "devout matron who took him as her boarder because she developed an ardent liking for the lad on account of his singing and heartfelt prayers in church." Dresser (1584) speaks of "a certain mother of a family" who gave him bread out of compassion. Rebhan (1621) refers to "a pious, wealthy widow" who gave Luther bread and took him into her house because of his singing and praying, but says that her name is unknown. Topp (1660) combines all the foregoing accounts, but still does not connect them by name with Ursula Cotta. The first to do so is Christian Franz Paullini, in his *Dissertationes historicae* of 1694: from a gravestone giving Ursula Cotta's death as 1511, Paullini concludes (on no good grounds) that the benefactress was the widow of Konrad Cotta, Ursula née Schalbe. Kessler points out the flaws in Paullini's harmonization, which has been followed by Luther biography ever since. While it is not impossible that the young Luther lodged with the Schalbes and boarded with the Cottas, there is no evidence that he did. The gravestone proves that there certainly was an Ursula Cotta, but it does not prove that she was married to Konrad. Ursula Cotta could not have been Konrad Cotta's widow when Luther was fourteen years old because Konrad was town guardian in 1505, toastmaster in 1510 and 1515, and died in 1525. Kessler then proceeds to reconstruct the true genealogy of the Cottas, which need not concern us here.

II

The fact of the matter may be less colorful but is far more revealing than the legend. The Lindemanns, Schalbes, and Cottas were all part of the same patrician circle of Eisenach burghers and were closely related.[21] They were leading citizens of the city, from whom its magistrates and municipal officers were drawn, and they held high educational ambitions and professional goals. It was here, among his mother's people and their values, that Martin Luther lived throughout the years of his early adolescence.

Apart from class and cultural aspirations which were confirmed during these years, the most explicit impression seems to have been left on the youth's religious experience. We have already noted Melanchthon's statement that Martin had been "diligently instructed at home in the knowledge and fear of God" as soon as he could understand, and also that Hanna's own "modesty, fear of God, and prayerfulness were especially obvious, and other upright women paid her close attention as an example of virtue."[22] We have also heard Rector Schneidewein compare Hanna's sanctity and wisdom to biblical models.[23] It has been fashionable to treat these testimonies as polite convention, or to suppose, as Heinrich Boehmer does, that "for her, too, 'prayer and grey hair' (*im Alter der Psalter*) quite possibly developed together."[24] But it seems altogether likely that Melanchthon and Schneidewein, who knew Hanna Luder well, were reporting quite accurately a piety which was characteristic of her and her Eisenach circle, and which did not fail to leave a lasting impression on her son.

For we have Luther's own evidence for the godliness of the people he lived and associated with in Eisenach. He identifies his host, Heinrich Schalbe, as an intimate and devotee of the Franciscans. This Heinrich Schalbe, who became mayor of Eisenach, was closely connected, and probably related by blood, to the Lindemann family. In Luther's first extant letter, inviting Vicar Braun of Eisenach to his first mass in Erfurt in 1507, he expresses gratitude to the "Schalbe College, those excellent people who from my point of view are as richly deserving as they could possibly be."[25]

It was from Heinrich Schalbe that the boy Luther heard about the old Franciscan visionary Johann Hilten.[26] In his declining years, Hilten was being kept in seclusion by his order at the retreat house of St. Elizabeth of Hungary, by the Wartburg outside Eisenach. Hilten had earlier been sent from Nürnberg as a missionary to Livonia, but there his charismatic and spiritualist activities had fomented a social scandal, and the magistrates of Riga had secured his removal.[27] Since Hilten belonged to the Observant (strict) branch of the Franciscan order, he seems to have been kept under virtual house arrest for the many years after his return from Livonia, lest his apocalyptic and spiritualizing views should give the Observants a reputation as enthusiasts. In their political struggle with their Conventual rivals, the Observants wished to avoid such controversy. However, Hilten's prophecies, as we saw, were later applied to Luther in the *Apology* to the Augsburg Confession; Luther underlined Hilten's name in red in his copy of the *Apology*, and wrote in the margin:

I think this man was still alive or recently dead when I was taking my first lessons in Eisenach. For I remember that mention was made of him by my host Heinrich Schalbe, who expressed compassion for his

51

being virtually bound in prison. I was 14 or 15. The same Heinrich Schalbe was an intimate of the Minorites, almost their captive and slave, with his whole family.[28]

The Observant Franciscans, to whom the Schalbe sodality was so devoted, maintained a cloister within Eisenach as well as the retreat house outside it.

Among this "college" of godly people in Eisenach, Vicar Braun, as we know from the warmth of Luther's two letters to him, became a close and beloved friend.[29] Braun's invitation to the first mass included an invitation to another cousin of Luther's, Conrad Hutter, who had been sacristan of St. Nicholas's Church in Eisenach. Potentially the most significant impact of the Lindemann circle on the spirituality of the adolescent Luther would have come from the sermons he heard when he attended church in their company. This is a matter of such importance that it will deserve separate treatment in a chapter of its own. But it is clear that the task of formation in godliness that began at his mother's knee was continued and crystallized in these years among his mother's kinsfolk.

III

Several difficulties surround the later reports of Luther's memory of first discovering a complete Bible in a library, to his great delight. Dietrich, Rörer, Lauterbach, and Mathesius all differ slightly as to whether Luther was a boy, an adolescent, a baccalaureus, or even a monk when the incident occurred, and whether it happened in the university or the cloister at Erfurt, or perhaps earlier.[30] Some biographers have found the whole incident unlikely. From the sources, the most probable time and place was the university library at Erfurt while Luther was preparing for his master's degree—that is, shortly before he entered the cloister. What is clear, however, is that the older Luther associated in memory the discovery of his beloved Bible with one story in particular: the story of Samuel's mother in 1 Samuel 1. It is surely no accident that the locus of his excitement and delight should be the story of a godly woman named Hannah who lent her son to the Lord for his whole life.

52

5

Harrowing the Heart:
The Preaching of Luther's Youth

At the extremely impressionable age of thirteen to seventeen years, in the midst of the tempestuous adolescent passage during which ideological attachments are so easily swayed, Martin Luther lived among his mother's family in Eisenach, and with these godly people went to church and listened to the preaching. It will give us new insight into Luther's religious formation if we can identify what he heard from the pulpits in that "nest of priests," his beloved Eisenach.

Of course we have no precise record of the very sermons he heard, or even the names of the preachers except for his friend Johann Braun, Vicar of St. Mary's Church. We may suppose, from the devotion of the Schalbe sodality to the Franciscan Observants, that sometimes he sat at the feet of Minorite preachers, whether residents of the monastery within the city or visitors to the retreat house of St. Elizabeth of Hungary below the Wartburg.

Regrettably, the style and content of the preaching to be heard in a city like Eisenach in the late 1490s has been virtually ignored. Plainly the preaching deserves study both for its own sake and for its place in the story of Luther and the Reformation. So we must turn our attention now to the impact of this preaching on the adolescent Luther. In order to do that, we must first pause to see how homiletic theology on the eve of the sixteenth century may be reconstructed. Then we will be in a position to recognize its decisive contributions to Luther's pilgrimage.

I

The historians' neglect of parochial preaching creates a critical gap in the study of Reformation backgrounds. In other respects, great effort has been expended on the medieval background of Luther's theology. In recent years, much needed descriptions have been given of the nominalist theology, espoused by some professors at Luther's alma mater, the University of Erfurt, and especially of the doctrines of Gabriel Biel, whose *Exposition of the Canon of the Mass* Luther was required to study for his ordination. The range of scholastic allegiances represented within Luther's own order, the Augustinian order, has been canvassed. Perhaps most useful of all, tne outlook of Luther's superior and mentor, Johann von Staupitz, has been thoroughly examined.[1]

A less fruitful side effect of this upsurge in interest in "the Reformation in medieval perspective" has been a rash of studies that comb every syllable of the writings of "young Luther" for esoteric clues to his knowledge of scholastic theology and his progress in separating from it. Such studies are based on the least adequate parts of Luther's output (works he himself called "a crude and inchoate muddle"[2]). They tend to mistake for theological innovation that freshness of mind and vitality of expression that were Luther's from the beginning. They consider the starting point of Luther's progress to be his commitment to scholastic doctrine, especially to Gabrielist nominalism, even though such an identification is impossible to prove and implausible in the face of the evidence. Above all, they make an elitist and intellectualizing assumption when they presume that the important background to Luther's revolution was academic theology. That is unlikely (to say the least) in Luther's own spiritual journey, and self-evidently false in the lives of those masses of lay people who received his message and made the Reformation a social reality.

Luther became a reformer out of urgent pastoral concern. The reality which evoked that concern was not a set of theological formularies but a religious culture. To be sure, Luther challenged the school theologians and fervently disputed their doctrines, which he knew with searching thoroughness; but his response was not for the sake of scholarly clarification. He was deeply and personally aware of the "meanings, modes and uses"[3] of penitence that flowed from prevailing doctrines to the people through all the channels of the churchly culture.

Accordingly, attention to the practical impact of sacramental confession on the lives of sincere lay Christians is a welcome corrective to a rarefied intellectualizing approach. Ozment has tellingly described the central place of penance in the propaganda of the early Reformation, in the flood of pamphlets which indicate so well the appeal of the new doctrine and the receptivity of the burghers of the imperial cities.[4] This material is an invaluable resource for the social history of the Reformation. Tentler has studied the theories and purposes of penance from the clergy's side in some confessors' manuals circulating on the eve of the Reformation,[5] but even these manuals remain somewhat academic until interpreted in actual penitential practice. The pastoral reality at the parochial level, and in the confessional itself, could be a far cry from the logic of scholarly summators.

It is here that neglect of the study of preaching in the pre-Reformation period has created such a gap. In the sermonic literature of the day we may find injunctions to penance, descriptions of uprightness and transgression, rules for improvement of life, exhortations to contrition, accounts of the harrowing of the heart, calculations of duty and threats of purgatory not in the careful and precise calculus of the learned, but "in simple language, not profundities"[6]—the language in which they were actually addressed to the people. This homiletic theology does more to flesh out the religious setting in the cities than all the disquisitions of the schools.

Why, then, has it been so largely ignored? An obvious answer is that it was swept aside by the overwhelming revival of preaching in the Reformation itself and by the disdain of Reformation preachers for their forerunners. It may be, too, that the rise of the printed book steadily reduced the reliance of earnest lay people on sermons for their religious instruction; by 1500 the compilation of model sermons for oral delivery to the people was already giving way to more literary modes of communication. Yet within the first decades of printing, some of the most popular items for printers and buyers were sermon books for the use of preachers. Massive collections of model sermons, postils, and exemplary illustrations were reprinted time after time and circulated in huge numbers.

These sermon books do little to justify the period's reputation as the nadir of the preaching tradition. Rather, the evidence suggests a new surge of attention to the preacher's responsibility. Conciliar sentiment, the growing Observant movement within the preaching orders, and the piety of the *devotio moderna* all included in their reforming energies a powerful commitment to thoroughness, excellence, and intelligibility in a preaching designed specifically for parochial use. The composition of such homiletic aids reached a peak in the first half of the fifteenth century, when sermon books circulated widely in manuscript; after the invention of printing, and especially between 1470 and 1500, this literature gained a second lease on life and a greatly expanded sphere of influence. Sermonic aids enjoyed a much wider circulation and use as printer after printer issued editions of the most popular collections. To take just four notable examples: the *Quadragesimale*, or Lenten series, of Johannes Gritsch, O.M. (fl. 1430), was printed twenty-nine times between 1475 and 1500 (twenty-four of those editions in Germany); the *Sermones dormi secure* of Johannes of Werden, O.M. (d. 1437) saw thirty-four editions before 1500, and nearly sixty more in the next half century; the thorough but anonymous *Sermones thesauri novi* were printed twenty-nine times between 1483 and 1497; and various sermon books by the most comprehensive author of all, the Nürnberger Dominican Johannes Herolt (d. 1468), went through at least sixty-four editions between 1470 and 1500 (one hundred and seventy-five editions, if the *Postil* of "Guillermus Parisiensis" is also attributable to Herolt).[7] By 1492, the humanist scholar Johannes Trithemius personally knew of more than thirty authors of his century who had produced complete sets of model sermons for the whole church year, and as many more who had written sermons for various occasions; and his list is far from exhaustive.[8] In short, we have an indispensable source for understanding the Christianity preached to the urban laity on the very eve of the Reformation.

The new classically inspired preaching styles that appeared during this period in Renaissance Italy were not rapidly adopted in the North.[9] Preaching in the North on the whole continued to adhere to the traditional rules of the *artes praedicandi,* the manuals of preaching method, but those rules simply created a conventional, empty structure whose success depended wholly on the preacher's skill in giving it content.[10] Within a shared outline, preaching styles varied widely. We may roughly distinguish several broad overlapping streams: first, sophisticated scholastic sermons, directed (like Gabriel Biel's) to a learned academic audience or (like Geiler von Keysersberg's or Johann Nider's) to cathedral congregations; secondly, popular mission sermons, made famous by such noteworthy practitioners and showmen as John of Capistrano, Bernardino of Siena, or Vincent Ferrer; thirdly, preaching within the cloisters to congregations of monks or nuns, especially devotional and sometimes mystical sermons (Heinrich Harp [d. 1477] is a notable exemplar); and fourthly, sermons specifically designed to be preached in a parochial situation, on a regular basis week by week, to congregations of lay people. Strangely, the first three categories are most often commented on, though the fourth—the parochial preaching—is by far the largest and most significant class, both in numbers and in influence.

To describe the method of the popular parochial sermon books is to indicate their importance. Most of these collections consist of model sermons or sermon outlines containing one or more sermons for each Sunday, holy day, and saint's day of the church year. Other sets contain daily sermons for Lent or Advent. They are usually written in Latin; they thus presume, as a minimum competence, the ability of the preacher who uses them to render them in the vernacular. Some authors, like Herolt and Werden, give German equivalents for uncommon or complicated Latin expressions, and on the whole the Latin is not demanding. Indeed, even though most of these sermons are explicitly designed for expansion and adaptation, they are sufficiently complete and self-contained to allow for simple translation if need be. Most contain thematic indexes, and some offer an additional index of encapsulated theme outlines which permit the preacher to piece together his own sermon by rearranging sections of the text. Gritsch's Lenten sermons, for example, may be adapted for Sunday use throughout the year by the use of such a table; and Herolt offers an index for creating saints' days sermons out of his *de tempore,* or Sunday, sermons.

The compilers make clear that they are deliberately avoiding scholastic subtleties and profundities, that they seek a simplicity that is edifying and appropriate to common folk, to the people, to the simple; and that their models are to be used by simple preachers who do not have the sophistication or the resources to devise their own instructive distinctions, locate telling authorities, or invent graphic images and exemplary stories. The very title of Johann of Werden's collection, the "Sleep Soundly Sermons," indicates this purpose:

Lord's Day sermons containing expositions of the gospels throughout the year, worthy of note and useful by all priests, pastors, and chaplains: called Sleep Soundly, or Sleep Without Anxiety, in that without great study they may be readily incorporated and adopted as a happy starting point for preaching to the people.[11]

Similarly, Johann Herolt prefaces his *de sanctis* sermons with the comment:

Although many sermons more replete with opinions and more cultivated in speech have been compiled by many illustrious doctors, yet for simple preachers it is sometimes more acceptable to study and preach simple things rather than profundities.[12]

While these collections vary considerably in the demands they make on the user, the sets that sold most widely were those that were pitched to ordinary parochial needs and accommodated the everyday exercise of pastoral care. On the whole, the scholastic *summae* and the decretals were cited only to give authority to practical moral instruction, rules of churchly discipline, or answers to questions of conscience from the laity. Otherwise, the sophisticated logic-chopping of scholastic method was avoided (or translated into pastoral simplicity).

On several grounds—the urban location of the author/collectors, the need for at least moderate Latin skills on the part of the preachers, and above all the content of the sermons—it is plain that the setting for which these preaching aids were designed and in which they were put to use was the parochial life of the cities. Most of the compilers whose careers are known were affiliated with mendicant houses in the cities. The requisite knowledge of languages and the capability (or even the right) to preach was exceptional in rural parishes, staffed as they so often were by a barely literate proletariat of supply priests. There was little concerted effort by the church to preach to the rural laity until the century after the Reformation, Catholic and Protestant. In content, though illustrations drawn from nature and farming are often used, the social milieu to which ethical instruction is offered is explicitly an urban population. The economy and class structure presumed is that of the cities. A high level of understanding and commitment is expected of at least some of the hearers, a response that the authors expected of townsfolk rather than peasants. Like Luther after them, their concern for simple Christians did not always reach as far as the "rough herd."

As to internal diversity within the body of sermonic literature, two different things must be said. Within the shared outlines of the *ars praedicandi*, these preachers differ very widely in style and interpretative method; but in spite of these wide variations of style, their homiletic theology is remarkably unanimous, both in its choice of themes and its treatment of them. Both style and content made their impress on the young Luther.

At the risk of oversimplifying, we may observe two main stylistic approaches to the art of communication. One style is didactic and explanatory: its use of scriptural proof texts and other authorities is fairly literal, and for illustration it depends chiefly on exemplary stories. The other style is more evocative and persuasive; it displays a great love for scripture, which it uses tropologically (that is, by allegories with direct pastoral application), and for illustration it employs symbols, especially allusive visual imagery, drawn from nature, the bestiaries, legend, or iconographical tradition. (Though it would certainly be a

mistake to identify a particular style with any one of the preaching orders, it may be safe to say that Dominican preachers
favored the didactic style, while Franciscans were the great ex-
ponents of the tropological style. There are notable exceptions
to this general rule, however.)

What is particularly noteworthy about this stylistic diversity
is its evidence of two distinct and alternative uses of scripture.
The secondary literature often gives the impression that the
expository device called the *Quadriga*, or fourfold sense, remained the normal method of interpreting scripture until it was
swept away by humanists and reformers in the sixteenth century. This ancient method distinguished the literal sense from
three sorts of allegorical or spiritual sense; the allegorical sense
proper (referring to Christ), the anagogical sense (referring to
the church or to the eschaton), and the tropological sense (referring to Christian faith and morals).[13] In practice, the situation
was both simpler and more complicated than this account. The
allegorical understanding did remain in use by many expositors,
but in practice it was the exception rather than the rule for all
four senses to be identified. Instead, preachers were wont to
identify the literal sense of a text very briefly and then move
directly to a simple tropological application introduced by the
words *ita moraliter* or *ita spiritualiter*. Alongside the traditional
allegorical method, however, a highly literalistic attitude to exposition was also in vogue before the Reformation. The literal
concern for the grammatical and historical meaning of the text
shown by the fourteenth-century exegetes Nicholas of Lyra, O.M.,
Nicholas of Gorran, O.P., and others was reproduced and imitated
throughout the fifteenth century. The most widely circulated
preacher's aid before 1500 was the pseudonymous *Postil of
Guillermus Parisiensis*, which enjoyed a staggering 110 incunabu-
lar editions (40,000 copies in a space of thirty years would be a
remarkable circulation in any age).[14] This work, which is an
edited version of manuscripts from the 1430s attributed to
Johann Herolt, is a spare word-by-word literal exegesis of the
texts of the epistles and gospels for the church year. The enor-
mous popularity of this book accords with the prevailing use of
a literal approach and avoidance of allegory by that preaching
style we have called "didactic."

Both Erasmus and Luther, in their early writings, declare themselves opposed to the mere literalism they saw espoused by many of their contemporaries. For paradoxically, those preachers who continued to search for spiritual meanings displayed a far livelier and more sensitive knowledge and love of the scriptures than their literalist colleagues. While the literalists tended to use scripture just as they used other authorities, as proof texts for systematic assertions, the allegorists more often developed their themes from the details of their text and with a devoted sense of the Bible's religious energies. The extraordinary richness of Luther's mature expository style—its emotional wealth, its abundance of figures, its amazing agility in finding verbal parallels—is much more continuous with the tropological than with the didactic preaching tradition.

In their doctrinal content, however, the sermon books do not display the same degree of divergence. In their choice of themes, and generally in their theological attitudes, they show a remarkable consistency. Some collections are so thorough that they treat a very broad array of issues, but amid a profusion of social, moral, sacramental, dogmatic, and eschatological topics, several themes emerge insistently as the predominant message of all this preaching. In terms of simple quantity, the call for uprightness of life and the ascetic and social-ethical implications of Christian faith are the most frequently sounded themes. But in terms of rhetorical power and pastoral emphasis, two other twin themes emerge as the central and all-controlling motifs: *memoria mortis,* the salutary awareness of death; and contrition, the character of true penitence.

It is not too much to say that these preachers teach a doctrine of justification by contrition alone. Most of the other perennial *loci* of medieval doctrine—grace, rewards and merits, venial and mortal sins, almsgiving and the works of holy mercy, the strict accounting of judgment, the intercession of the saints, the pains of purgatory and the horrors of hell—all are subsumed in practice to the essential pastoral goal of evoking contrition; and the inescapable reality of death, at once the most certain and the most uncertain fact of life, is the pervading context for that penitence.

While there were growing tensions among scholarly theologians about how penance worked, the preachers spoke with one voice to the people. Among the academic writers of confessors' manuals the "contritionist" view of Peter Lombard and Thomas Aquinas (which located the efficacy of penance in the prior sincerity of the contrite heart) was steadily modified by a Scotist emphasis on the sacramental efficacy of the priest's role. Almost without exception, the message conveyed by the sermon books promotes the older, contritionist belief that sincere repentance brings God's forgiveness before and apart from sacramental penance, given only that the penitent firmly intends to make confession and satisfaction both as a mark of sincerity and in obedience to church precept. Accordingly, there is an overwhelming emphasis on the need for deepest sincerity and humble self-examination.

Whatever else the hearers of sermons around 1500 took from their preachers, we may be sure that the paired themes of contrition and death were never allowed to escape their attention. To the sincere and godly person who earnestly sought the favor of God and salvation, the urgency of availing oneself of all the churchly means of grace was made inescapably plain. The preachers knew that the number of lay people who would actually live out in the world all their austere injunctions to mortification was tiny—one in thirty thousand, one preacher guessed —though such extreme devotion did appear (as the spiritual autobiography of the English laywoman Margery Kempe, for example, gives evidence[15]). A more realizable goal was to lead earnest parishioners into sincere conformity to ecclesial discipline, a fervent desire for grace, an active commitment to such spiritual exercises as fasting, bodily castigations, pilgrimage, meditation on the passion, devotion to the blessed Virgin, membership in religious brotherhoods, and perhaps (in a few, but most highly valued, cases) conversion to the religious life.

There is every reason to believe that the response of many citizens of the imperial cities to these exhortations was active, heartfelt, and anxiously seeking. Vincenz Hasak rightly says, "The fact is that in that time too there was much Christian faith, much Christian hope, much Christian love, much Christian life in German lands, in German families, in German hearts." There was at least as frequent preaching then as now, he points out, and attendance at sermons was held to be a Christian's most serious duty.[16]

II

It must be obvious by now how crucially such doctrine would affect a Martin Luther. He was by nature an extremely committed, impassioned, and ardent youth, scrupulously raised by a pious mother and an ambitious father, and in the care of an admired circle of devout and influential relatives. Young Martin provided well-prepared and fertile soil for the preached word. One incident gives us some idea of the graphic impact of mendicant spirituality on the impressionable teenager even before he went to Eisenach. Luther later recalled:

With my own eyes I saw, when I was at school in Magdeburg in my fourteenth year, a Duke of Anhalt who went abroad in the streets in barefoot monks' garb begging bread and lugging his sack like an ass so that he was forced to stoop to the ground. . . . They had so benumbed him that he carried out every task in the cloister just like any monk, and had so devoted himself to fasting, vigils, and castigations that he looked like a death mask, mere skin and bone. And he was soon buried, for he was too weak to sustain so strenuous a life.[17]

One insistent theme of the preaching, we have seen, was the memory of death. In a typical allegorizing of the parable of the sower, Johann of Werden likens the soul of the Christian to a field: "As any farmer works his field so that it will yield fruit, so every man should work his heart and body." After the farmer plows his field, he spreads manure; so after the harrowing of the heart by contrition and confession, the Christian must apply spiritual fertilizer:

We must enrich the field of our body and heart with the manure of the memory of death so that it will yield fruit (Ecclus 7). . . . For what will man be after death? Surely manure and ashes, cinders and clay (Job 30). And a person must keep these things constantly in mind. . . . Death does not tarry. Let a man think of the deaths of our predecessors when they were strong—Absalom at his most beauteous.

63

David at his boldest, Solomon at his wisest, Samson at his strongest. They all passed and reverted to earth.[18]

The terrible thing about natural death, Werden says in a sermon on the fourfold death (of nature, of guilt, of spirit, and of hell), is that all men fall under its domination and receive its sentence; the horrible vision of demons awaiting the soul accompanies it; it is dire in its dissolution of all our members; and it issues in a fearful assessment of all our works without chance of repentance.[19] And in a powerful Ash Wednesday homily, Werden lists death as an urgent reason to be turned to God with the whole heart:

I say that a man must be converted on account of the uncertainty of death; whence Bernard: "Nothing is more certain than death and nothing more uncertain than the hour of death." And the poet says:
hoc scio, quod morior, ubi quomodo nescio quando
Often a man falls unprepared into the pit of death when he is not expecting it. There is an *exemplum* in "On the nature of things" about a certain man who was walking through the desert, and a unicorn charged at him trying to kill him with its horn, almost piercing the man's heart; and as the man was backing away, defending his front as well as he could, he fell over backwards into a very deep pit. In the midst of the pit a tree was growing, on which he became caught in his fall. Under it, in the bottom of the pit, there were serpents and toads rearing their heads waiting for him to fall. Then out from the walls there came two mice, one white and one black, who together started gnawing at the tree. On the tree itself there were beautiful apples growing, so he picked the apples and ate and all his grief was wiped from his mind—the unicorn standing above, the toads and serpents below, and the mice gnawing away—until the tree fell, he tumbled into the pit, and the serpents and toads devoured him. *Ita moraliter:* the "unicorn" is death, which is horrible, sparing no one, neither rich nor poor, neither old nor young, seeking to slay man. But man defends himself from it as best he can. And when he feels the "unicorn" come—that is, death—he swiftly seeks a remedy for death. The "pit" is the grave in which sit serpents and toads awaiting man's death; but man "sits in a tree" of human frailty, at which "two mice gnaw"—that is, day and night (day is white, night is black). But the "apples" in the tree are the delights of this world which a man consumes and forgets death and the frailty of his nature,

64

until he falls into the pit of the grave and is devoured by serpents and toads. So we must be converted quickly; for we do not know when death is coming.[20]

Medieval preaching had long before gathered a catena of warnings on the inevitability and unpredictability of death, from Gregory, Bede, Isidor, and above all Bernard. These authorities are all quoted by the *Sermones thesauri novi* in impressing on Christians the urgent need for preparation for death, because of its uncertainty, the ensuing examination in judgment, and the accompanying temptation by demons.[21] To this standard catalogue of motives is often added a rather gruesome account of the body's death agony, together with the spiritual analogues of each stage of the struggle.

Johannes Gritsch, whose preaching is marked by its careful (if somewhat studied) use of balanced mnemonic *distinctiones*, lists the certainty of death as one of five allurements to heaven and inducements to penance—consideration of one's own bliss, the severity of judgment, the opportunity for grace, uncertainty of one's status before God, and certitude of the peril of death:

For our life is the swiftest rush towards death: in it we are not permitted to stand still for a moment or slow down. . . . Since, then, the sinner is careening towards death like this, the Lord often comes to meet him and tells him through inspiration to reflect how he has been adjudged to an eternal punishment, to which he is being driven without pause. So the Lord says "Grieve that you have committed sin and killed your soul." If, then, the sinner shall say, "I grieve from my heart," immediately he is freed by the Lord from hanging in hell and is reconciled to God. . . . Behold the revocation of the sentence of death![22]

In another *distinctio*, Gritsch says that death is threefold: *corporalis et meditanda, spiritualis et fugienda, Gehennalis et timenda* (physical—to be meditated on; spiritual—to be fled; hellish—to be feared). And he goes on to stress the salutary fruits of meditating on death: "Meditation on the first death avails to many ends: to contempt of the world, to self-humiliation, to a flight from sin, to ruling one's life, to doing penance, and to the desire for life eternal."[23] Johannes Herolt agrees: "He who daily remembers that he will die despises the present and hastens to the future."[24]

In such exhortations we hear spelled out the purposes that drove Martin Luther, as a graduate student at Erfurt, to abandon the study of law (and his father's professional ambitions for him) and to enter the religious life; and it is certainly no accident that Luther's fateful entrance to the cloister was preceded by a series of close brushes with the fact and with the threat of death.

Though we have only scant information about Luther's brothers and sisters (and most of it from later years), it was all but inevitable that one or more younger siblings died in infancy during Luther's student years. We do know that two younger brothers died of the plague just after Luther was priested, and this somewhat reconciled Hans Luder to his oldest son's profession.[25] Plague was a recurrent peril and a normal fact of life.

Luther was himself directly threatened by the prospect of sudden death. On one of his walking visits from Erfurt to his home in Mansfeld, probably in 1503, he was dangerously wounded:

Intending to return to his home county, as he began his journey he accidently slashed his leg on his sword—the blade slipped out and he impaled himself on it. The sword ruptured the cephalic artery. He was alone in the field except for one companion, as far from Erfurt as Eutzsch is from Wittenberg (half a mile). There the blood poured out profusely and he could not stand up, so he lay on his back and put his leg in the air, and pressed his finger on the wound. The leg swelled to an astounding size. Eventually a doctor was brought from the city and dressed the wound. As he waited, he was in danger of death, and said: "O Mary, help!" ("I would have died there upon Mary!" he said). Later that night, in bed, the wound hemorrhaged again; as he faded, again he invoked Mary.[26]

There is an undated reference to a similar accident befalling one of his brothers, who cut a vein in a knee and was near death.[27]

Melanchthon, explaining the occasion for Luther's conversion to the religious life, reports Luther as saying that when he thought earnestly about the wrath of God or about wondrous examples of punishments "he sometimes was suddenly smitten by such terrors that he almost expired. . . . He felt these terrors either for the first time, or at any rate most sharply, in that year when he lost a friend who died for I know not what cause."[28]

But Luther's most famous brush with death, and the event that immediately precipitated his entrance to the Black Cloister, was a thunderstorm in which he was caught at Stottenheim. After graduation as a master of arts in February 1505, he had spent the spring recess before beginning the study of law in a troubled state of introspective sadness, of *tentatio tristitiae* over his spiritual status. Then in June he took an unaccountable leave from his classes to visit his parents in Mansfeld, again on foot. As he approached Erfurt on his way back, he was so terrified by a thunderbolt that he cried out in terror and vowed, "Help me, St. Anna, and I will become a monk!"[29]

In the preaching of his youth, he would have heard that atmospheric disturbances were special messengers from God to remind human beings of sudden death and to urge them to seek God's mercy and grace. Church bells were traditionally rung during thunderstorms to remind men of this very message. Herolt declares that God sends storms

so that he may smite sinners with terror, and thus at last they may be converted. . . . Why are the bells rung against the tempestuousness of the air? . . . So that men hearing the peals may be provoked to call upon God lest he drown us on account of our sins as he drowned the whole world when the flood came. Therefore, when men hear the peal of the bells against the storms of the sky, whether by day or by night, they must fear for themselves, and humbly call upon God to deal mercifully with us.[30]

In terrified response to the voice of God in the storm, and in search of that mercy, Martin Luther entered the convent at Erfurt.

III

There is ample evidence of the struggles with penance that preoccupied the young monk within the cloister. So closely do the turmoils of his search for peace with God agree with the preachers' accounts of the harrowing of the contrite heart that he could virtually be said to have done just what was enjoined from so many pulpits.

Since the nature of true contrition is the all-pervading theme of this preaching on the eve of the Reformation, we can review here only the merest sample of these injunctions. But in the conversion of the sinner, the preachers agree, "contrition is our spiritual conception."[31]

The requirements of true penance, the *Sermones thesauri novi* tell us, are four: a firm intention not to sin further or to backslide; a reverential fear of God (for "there is no justification without fear"); shame, "the greatest part of penitence"; and grief for one's sins. "This is the way in which a man must needs turn back to his own heart morning and evening, to harrow his conscience and to wipe out his sin."[32] Grief over sins, Herolt says, is the work of the Holy Spirit in beginners on the spiritual way; frequent self-examination is the Spirit's work in proficients.[33] The cleansing of the soul is effected by frequent outpourings of tears.[34]

Is it possible for this grief to be excessive? Confessors were graphically aware of the pastoral problem of overscrupulousness. Johannes Gritsch gives a somewhat technical answer:

There are two sorts of sorrow involved in an act of penance: one is the grief of the rational will, repudiating its sin, and this is effectual in penance—there cannot be too much of this sorrow. But there is another sort of sorrow over sin not effectual in penance, and it takes two forms: first, grief inflicted on the body by a man's sins themselves; and secondly, an inward grief of the "sensitive appetite," caused by loss of wholeness or of glory by one's sins. Some say it can be excessive, others that it cannot because so exceeding a cause could not have too exceeding an effect. But such violent grief can so disrupt the harmony of the body that a suicidal passion results; so I agree with those who say that there can be excessive sorrow in the sensitive appetite.[35]

Even these technicalities make clear that a deep and pervasive sorrow for sin was assumed to be the normal mark of the penitent.

Furthermore, despair of one's own capacities was at the heart of contrition. God gives us the kingdom of heaven from his mercy, Herolt says,

for he is scarcely obliged to us on account of our merits—indeed, we do nothing worthy of him [*immo nihil de condigno*]. For if we achieve anything of good, yet we are bound to do more towards God. So even if we have consumed all the powers of body and soul in God's service, and have acted to the limits of our capacity, yet we must still say what Luke 17 says: "We are unprofitable servants: we have done what was our duty to do." That we cannot possess eternal life from our own merits in a worthy way [*ex condigno*], but only from God's mercy, Bernard shows when he says: "If we had been born from the moment man first appeared on earth and if our life were stretched out for a hundred thousand years, yet there would be no action of this whole time worthy to be compared to the future glory to be revealed in us."[36]

God's acceptance of man to grace, Werden says, is a greater miracle than creation, because creation happened without help and also without resistance, but we must be involved in our acceptance. Yet the help of the sinner consists solely in saying these four words in contrition of heart: "Peccavi, Domine, miserere mei."[37] True contrition is infused by God alone—"a man can confess and weep, yet have no true contrition unless God infuses it."[38]

As to the manner of true contrition, Werden allegorizes the Exodus in a sermon for the first Sunday in Lent. As Moses led the children of Israel out of Egypt into the desert, so Christ by inspiration leads sinners out of "Egypt," the state of sin, "dividing the waters" of penitence with the "rod" of the holy cross. And we must walk the twelve ways of the "desert" of penitence so that we may "enter the land of promise" eternal. The ways of contrition are these: contrition is so bitter that you remember every season of your life in bitterness—"all the days, all the years you have uselessly wasted." Second, your contrition must be universal, so you recognize how great a sinner you are—like David, who though he offended only once yet said, "I have sinned more than the sand of the sea and my sins are more than the multitude of the stars." Contrition, too, must be specific, and deal in turn with each particular sin that calls forth your sorrow. And it must be continual—every recollection of sins past must evoke a renewed act of contrition. In this desert of penitence, the contrite heart is infested with the bites of the serpent, the devil, in the guise of evil suggestions, distractions, and thoughts. "But whomever the craft of Satan bites, let him look to Christ hanging on the cross and seek favor, and the bite of the serpent will not harm him."[39]

In sermon after sermon, throughout the whole of this age and time, this call to utter sincerity and constant, searching sorrow for sin was sounded again and again and again. It seemed to offer to the young Luther a promise of spiritual rebirth and a surcease from fear that he tumultuously yearned to achieve. He found that instead of peace with God, it led to despair: "I was never able to be consoled about my baptism: 'Oh, how can one become pious even once?' And so I became a monk."[40] But even in the monastery, he could never be sure that he had attained what the preachers demanded: that pure contrition, motivated not by fear of loss but by desire for God, that God alone could infuse, in an unalloyed sorrow that the Spirit alone could evoke.

Luther's struggle to redefine repentance and to move beyond a doctrine of justification by contrition, of salvation by sincerity, to a personally liberating doctrine was driven forward not so much by the abstruse formularies of the schoolmen as by the potent and insistent appeals of the preachers.

IV

The sermon books of the late fifteenth century provide us with an explicit image of the religious outlooks and ideals enjoined upon the godly in the cities of Germany before the Reformation. Devout, strict, and prayerful people like Hanna Luder and Heinrich Schalbe took care to instruct their young folk in the fear of God, and the religious culture they passed on, the model of sincerity and meaning they themselves embodied, revolved around the mendicants' characteristic themes: the duties of the virtues, accountability before God, the nature of true contrition, an austere spirituality of humiliation, awe of the supernatural, and the ever-present consciousness of death.

6

His Mother's God

Our quest for Luther's mother has led to several factual corrections of the received tradition. We also have a significantly revised basis for judging Luther's family background, social class, and cultural outlook; his family's fortunes during his childhood; the circumstances of his years at school in Eisenach; his mother's role in his early development and spiritual formation; and the elements of his decision to enter the religious life.

Is there, finally, any other evidence, besides the circumstances of family connection and the testimony of Luther's friends, to suggest the strong influence upon him of his mother Margarethe? Are we in a stronger position to assess Erik Erikson's statement that "we had better prepare ourselves . . . for an almost exclusively masculine story"?

I

Martin Luther is one of those historic figures who have been recast by each generation in its own image. There is now even a substantial literature reviewing Luther historiography and the extent to which images of Luther have mirrored his biographers' ideological commitments. As Ernst Zeeden says, "The changing picture of Luther through the decades and centuries has one constant factor, in that it is a reflex of religious ideas."[1] Jaroslav Pelikan wryly remarks, "To the gallery of earlier portraits our century has added Luther the Nazi, Luther the Kierkegaardian, and Luther the Barthian, while some American Protestants, in

mistaken zeal, have tried to draw a picture of Luther the Jeffer-
sonian."[2] This process has continued in our own generation.
Roland Bainton's *Here I Stand,* with its deft, winsome narrative
of a brave and conscientious individual refusing to bow before
ideological tyranny, was produced in the midst of the McCarthy
era in America.[3] And given the preoccupation of the mid-
twentieth-century West with self-awareness, it is no accident that
the most popular subsequent treatment has been Erikson's *Young
Man Luther: A Study in Psychoanalysis and History.*

With characteristic wit and accuracy, Gordon Rupp has described Erikson's book as "the most intelligent essay on Luther
in English of our time . . . brilliant but one-sided and entirely
unconvincing."[4] It is a brilliant book: it has asked new questions
of Luther biography that genuinely enrich our understanding,
and some of the criticism of the book has done it less than jus-
tice by concerning itself with details or misconstruing Erikson's
purpose. Yet, on the focal issue of Luther's relation to his parents,
it does remain unconvincing because (perhaps inevitably) it
deals with only half the story.

For in light of what we now know about Hanna Luder, the
psychological picture of a jealous, overbearing father who so
interfered in Hanna's mothering of Martin that she was virtually
eclipsed[5] becomes less plausible. True, Erikson does infer from
the scant evidence that "she must have provided him with a font
of basic trust on which he was able to draw in his fight for a primary faith."[6] Yet psychoanalysis has had an ingrained predilec-
tion for confining maternal influence to the earlier, nurturing
stages of development and stressing the father's influence in the
later, ideological stages. In this case, it seems implicit in Erikson's reconstruction that to struggle with a jealous, demanding
God is to deal with a paternal presence; but the God with whom
Martin Luther had to deal was his mother's God.

In support of his masculine version of the case, Erikson claims
that in Luther's story women in general have an extremely limited role, there are echoes of deep disappointment by the mother
in Luther's treatment of women, and the Mother of God is de-
throned.[7] This is not the place to embark on a thoroughgoing
exposition of Luther's reflections on women, let alone the long-

term effects of the Reformation on their status. But Erikson's observations on this score are simply not reliable.[8] It may be true that, in the alliance of Protestantism and the bourgeoisie, the role of Christian housewife became an institution which reduced women to an instrumental and ancillary function, and effectively curtailed any practical working equality with men. Luther probably encouraged that process by repeating traditional male canards about the frailty of women and their incapacity outside the domestic sphere.[9] But within his severely limited horizons, there is no doubt he intended to enhance the respect accorded women, especially by contrast with the contemporary fashion among academic humanists of waxing eloquent about female pulchritude while scornfully and contemptuously ridiculing women as worthless.[10] He repeatedly attacked those who disdained women as inferior or as necessary evils for blaspheming the creation of God, who made women and men equally human and noble, and equally bearers of the image of God.[11] When his biblical text provided him an image of a strong woman, his exposition took on a special liveliness.[12] And it is certainly not the case that Luther refers to the Virgin Mary "almost sneeringly";[13] true, she is not mediator instead of, alongside, or (worst of all) between us and Christ, but she has "all honor, all blessedness, and a unique place in all humankind, amongst whom she has no equal."[14]

Although Luther's conscious ideas about women remained to some extent bound by sixteenth-century cultural fetters, the evidence before us does not portray a psychic reality that was "almost exclusively masculine." The ignoring of Hanna Luder creates the greatest difficulty in Erikson's account.

We may remark in passing that a psychohistorical essay is especially vulnerable to such lacunae. In addition to the intrinsic difficulties of method involved in analyzing an absent and unresponding subject, there is moreover a particular risk of projecting back onto another age and culture the preoccupations of our own. For example, our own experience of the mobility and independence of the generations creates in our psychology a preoccupation with the adolescent task of separating from parents—a concern that may have limited relevance in a more settled and interdependent family culture where parental honor is highly valued (Luther certainly regarded "Honor thy father and mother" as binding throughout the parents' lifetime). Or to take another example: it is tempting (in our genteel and sanitary age) to place much psychological store by Luther's many anal references, but he lived in a time when such scatological language was commonplace and excrement was an undisguised fact of life. We must be cautious of too neat or schematic a pattern of interpretation: our analytic suggestions can be only partial, since all psychological events have many roots and serve many purposes.

II

Hans Luder's career was an upwardly mobile one. He came from the ranks of the upper peasantry, but (like other older sons in rural Thuringia) could not inherit his family farm and was forced to choose between sinking to the status of cottager or seeking an occupation elsewhere. In the course of entering the thriving silver-mining industry, he married into the bourgeoisie: his wife Margarethe belonged to the respected, influential, and highly educated old Eisenach family Lindemann. Martin Luther was aware at first hand of both his father's and his mother's ancestral homes.

Within the social status afforded by his marriage and commercial success, Hans Luder assumed the same sorts of educational and professional ambitions for his oldest son that his wife's relations held for their children. He made his own the Lindemanns' particular suggestion that the law and public office were the proper directions for a gifted and eloquent youth like Martin.

This suggestion emerged during an extended period in which Martin lived and worshiped and went to school among his mother's kinsfolk in Eisenach. Consider the psychological raw materials this stay provided for his adolescent passage: it was a setting of evident social success, status, and influence, where higher education and public leadership were valued and aspired to, and where he himself was encouraged and made much of. It was also a setting of sincere and devout spirituality, prayer, and attendance at sermons—a rigorous induction into a religious culture which had begun in his infancy, and now, in adolescence, among his mother's impressive family, encouraged in him an intense self-examination, an ethic of self-abnegation, and a lively fear of death and judgment.

The young man who emerged from this situation was confronted with two highly charged ideals, which at length came into deep conflict—the promise of public attainment, and the hunger for total commitment. He angered his father when, after a long period of inner turmoil, he could not reconcile the two and opted for dedication of his life to holiness. To his father, the way of manliness consisted in following the same upward path that he had taken, and traveling much farther along it. But the noteworthy thing is this: both ideals were indelibly associated with the mother's side of the young Luther's universe, in her own person and in the culture and influence of her family. Though it must remain a matter of pure conjecture, it is perhaps not too fanciful to suppose that Hanna's devotion was inwardly rewarded and pleased by her son's conversion to the religious life. At any rate, it is inconceivable that we should find in Martin Luther a story of personal development lacking the impress of either his father or his mother.

III

Karl Holl, in a brilliant essay, speaks of a "tension between elation and self-indictment" that was an enduring strand of Luther's personality; yet he insists that it represents no jarring or inconstancy in Luther himself.[15]

In his maturity, Martin Luther was a man of manifest greatness, yet undisguisedly stamped with our common humanity; an unusually complex man with a childlike love of simplicity; sensitive to the very edge of normalcy, yet unswerving in the face of enmity and mortal fear; warmhearted to the point of gullibility in the presence of need, but fierce to the point of abusiveness in the defense of truth. He was by turns (and sometimes at once) gentle and bawdy, witty and compassionate, clownish and sublime. Of brilliant mind and passionate soul, he feared his own mildness and native courtesy more than his outspoken reproof of error, yet he castigated himself in secret for causing his antagonists pain. He was a master of language, but he found his own creations a burden and hoped they would be forgotten. He was a zealot in defense of the authority of his office, but vehemently repudiated any authority in Luther the man. His path to greatness had to surmount huge obstacles. He was so nearly trapped by pathological self-doubt; he might have settled cheaply for a soothing local celebrity. Two self-assessments struggled within him: the image of a helpless, wretched beggar, and the image of a richly endowed champion of Christ. He became the reformer because he was able to hold both images in salutary tension—the mark of a hard-won but deep-seated wholeness.

Inevitably, that equilibrium gains spontaneous expression in his language; and there is one expression of it that is specially relevant to our concerns here. There is a quite remarkable balancing of masculine and feminine archetypes in Luther's imagery, and above all at the heart of his teaching, in his christological imagery.

Such archetypes, however widespread, perhaps arise only in the process of socialization. So in order to avoid anachronism, we must remain with those images of maleness and femaleness which belong to Luther's own psychosocial furniture. To a large extent, they are quite conventional. It is natural, he says,

for all mothers to be pleased by placid and unassuming dispositions and behavior; for women, who are good and honorable, are by nature diffident and gentle. . . . There is an innate difference between the dispositions of sons and daughters: the males are endowed with more ferocious personalities; daughters are more amiable, and do their parents' bidding more affably and sweetly.[16]

The great dignity and the highest good of the female sex is the life-giving gift of motherhood. Motherhood "reduces all evils to nothing . . . it is the divine blessing and mandate through which God preserves the whole human race in life."[17] Evidently, we should expect no great redefinition of masculinity and femininity in Luther's archetypes. Yet within these inherited boundaries, the intuitive search for balance between them is striking.

IV

We may begin with the balance between activity and passivity in Luther's description of faith. "Faith is and must be a steadfastness of the heart—it does not wobble, waver, quake, flutter or falter, but it stands firm and is sure of its rights."[18] "This faith stands firm in life and death, in hell and heaven, and nothing can overthrow it."[19] "Oh what a living, energetic, active, mighty thing is this faith."[20] "Is not faith an almighty, inexpressible thing that it can stand firm against such mighty enemies and gain victory?"[21] But this heroic image of a warrior faith is balanced by explicitly feminine images of the receptivity of faith: "True faith with outstretched arms joyfully embraces the Son of God given for it, and says, My beloved is mine and I am his."[22] "Faith holds the hand out and the sack open and lets him do nothing but good. . . . It is given only when you open your mouth, or rather your heart, and hold still and let yourself be filled."[23] "Faith is a very tender, precious thing, and easily injured."[24] But for Luther these two contrasting archetypes are perfectly integrated in the living act of faith: "True faith is a sheer work of God in us without any of our doing. . . . Thus it is also a very mighty, active, restless, busy thing."[25] "Faith is a lively and potent thing. . . . It is an industrious, stubborn and powerful thing, and if we would understand it aright, it is rather a passion than an action."[26] "Faith embraces Christ as a ring grasps a jewel."[27] On a subtler level, too, a transparent openness to the "maternal" side of human experience appears in the sensuousness of the imagery of faith, and in Luther's fascination with the unity of opposites. These themes appear graphically in that most feminine of all his writings, the *Magnificat* commentary, where he speaks of the divine dialectic of the heights and depths,[28] of "all the senses floating in God's love," of being "saturated by divine sweetness," of experience preceding understanding and "tasting before seeing."[29] Luther's baptismal and eucharistic writings are full of parallels.

Faith's double aspect corresponds to a twofold way in which Christ is given to us, as gift and example,[30] and to the parallel contrast between the fruit and the use of Christ's accomplishment: *fructus imitari, usus credere.*[31] The imagery that crowds around these distinctions maintains a balance between the "feminine" archetypes of submissiveness, earthiness, immanence, nurture, ecstasy and the "masculine" archetypes of initiative, transcendence, direction, cognition. Yet because Luther's emphasis in justification is on the unique sufficiency of Christ's work and our utter helplessness, it may seem at first as if his effort is to overcome the threatening, angry aspect of the Father-God by total absorption into maternal passivity and nurture. But this is not the whole story. The integration between father- and mother-identified elements is much closer, and it appears nowhere more clearly than in Luther's portrait of Christ himself.

On the one hand, Luther takes over from the patristic tradition very graphic language about Christ the slayer of sin and devourer of death, the victor over devil and hell and all tyrants. He is the hero-figure acting "under a special star." He is the leader and guide, the sun of righteousness, the lord over all creation.[32] But alongside these cosmic, martial, regal, and aggressive themes is an even richer strain of images of intimacy and nurture. Luther's favorite image for Christ is the brood-hen: "Look at the hen and her chickens and you will see Christ and yourself painted and depicted better than any painter could picture them."[33] He nourishes us with his strength as a hen feeds her chickens and warms them with her own body.[34] Christ is faith's jewel, "my heart's crown, my heart's joy, my ruby."[35] He is an inexhaustible fountain of living waters.[36] Scripture speaks richly of the maternal mercy of Christ, in which he cherishes and bears us just as a mother cherishes her tiny child and caresses it.[37]

Luther felt absolutely no inconsistency in combining in Christ, the embodiment of human perfection, strength and tenderness, dominion and nurture, majesty and intimacy—in short, all that collective and individual experience had identified as "masculine" and "feminine" characteristics. Moreover, if the dialectic of his early theology struggled to reconcile the "No!" of the hidden, patriarchal God with the "Yes!" of the gospel, in his mature teaching God encountered outside of Christ is not God as he really is: only the man Jesus is the *Kern und Ausbund* of God as he is. Thus the perfect coalescence of maternal and paternal roles that we find in Christ is also our access to the very being of God: "Even if you are feeble and soil yourself like an infant or an invalid, God will not summarily thrust you away, but he will always clean you and make you better."[38] God is pictured to us as the mother who is pregnant with us, who has given birth to us, who is nursing us.[39] He is at once the father who chastises us and the mother who caresses.[40]

"He shows his fatherly love toward us by the gentleness with which he adapts his speech to us, as a father with his children, taking delight in our childish patter and our faltering attempts to learn."[41] "Ask what you want unconcernedly, as a child with its father, who is pleased by everything the child does, so long as it clings to him."[42] "A mother's heart and love cannot forget her children—it is against nature. She would go through fire for her children. See how much labor women expend on making food, giving milk, keeping watch over a child: God compares himself to that passion. 'I will not desert you, for I am the womb that bore you, and I cannot let you go.' "[43]

The tenderness, strength, and delight of this picture of God, both mother and father, give eloquent testimony to the inner resources Martin Luther inherited, not only from Hans, but from Hanna Luder.

Abbreviations

References to Luther's writings are cited from the Weimar edition of his works by volume, page, line, and/or number:

WA   *D. Martin Luthers Werke.* Kritische Gesamtausgabe. Weimar, 1883– .

WA, Br   *D. Martin Luthers Werke.* Briefwechsel. Weimar, 1930– .

WA, DB *D. Martin Luthers Werke.* Deutsche Bibel. Weimar, 1906–1961.

WA, Tr *D. Martin Luthers Werke.* Tischreden. Weimar, 1912–1921.

Other Abbreviations

ADB   *Allgemeine deutsche Biographie.*

Copinger Walter A. Copinger, *Supplement to Hain's Repertorium bibliographicum, or collections towards a new edition of that work,* 2 pts. London: Henry Sotheran, 1895–1902.

CR   *Corpus Reformatorum,* ed. C. G. Bretschneider and H. E. Bindseil. Halle, 1834–1860.

Hain   Ludwig F. T. Hain, *Repertorium bibliographicum in quo libri omnes ab arte typographica inventa usque ad annum M.D.; typis expressi ordine alphabetico vel simpliciter enumerantur vel adcuratius recensentur. Indices uberrimi C. Burger.* Leipzig: Harrassowitz, 1891.

Reichling Dietrich Reichling, *Appendices ad Hainii-Copingeri Repertorium Bibliographicum. Additiones et emendationes,* 7 pts. Monachii: J. Rosenthal, and Monasterii Guestphalorum: Theissinger, 1905–14.

Notes

NOTES TO CHAPTER 1

1. Erik H. Erikson, *Young Man Luther: A Study in Psychoanalysis and History* (New York: W. W. Norton & Co., Inc., 1958), p. 71.
2. Augustine, *Confessions* 9.8.
3. *WA* 43, 676, 18.
4. Susanna Wesley, letter to John Wesley, quoted in John Kirk, *The Mother of the Wesleys: A Biography* (London: Jarrold, 1864), p. 159. See also the prayer of 17 May 1711, from the Headingly MSS of the writings of Susanna Wesley (Wesley College, Bristol) MSS A, fol. 65–6, printed in John A. Newton, *Susanna Wesley and the Puritan Tradition in Methodism* (London: Epworth Press, 1968) p. 111.
5. Heinrich Boehmer, *Road to Reformation*, trans. John W. Doberstein and Theodore G. Tappert (Philadelphia: Fortress Press, 1946), p. viii; German: *Der junge Luther*, 2d ed. (Leipzig: Koehler, 1939).
6. Robert H. Fife, *Young Luther: The Intellectual and Religious Development of Martin Luther to 1518* (New York: Macmillan Co., 1928), pp. 23–24.
7. Erikson, *Young Man Luther*, p. 72.
8. B. K. Kuiper, *Martin Luther: The Formative Years* (Grand Rapids, Mich.: Eerdmans, 1933), pp. 21–22.
9. *WA* 38, 338, 6–7.
10. Erikson, *Young Man Luther*, p. 72.
11. *WA* 48, 249.
12. *WA*, Tr 2, 376: #2250.
13. H. E. Jacobs, *Martin Luther, The Hero of the Reformation 1483–1546* (New York: G. P. Putnam's Sons; London: Knickerbocker, 1902), p. 7.
14. *WA*, Tr 5, 254: #5571.
15. *WA*, Tr 3, 415: #3566.
16. *WA*, Tr 2, 134: #1559.
17. *WA*, Tr 3, 131: #2982b.
18. Ibid.

19. WA, Tr 5, 139: #5428.

20. WA, Tr 2, 167: #1659; Tr 3, 213: #3181b.

21. E.g., David Richter, *Genealogia Lutheranorum* (Berlin: Rüdiger, 1733); Otto Sartorius, *Die Nachkommenschaft D. Martin Luthers* (Göttingen: Verlag der Lutheriden-Vereinigung, 1926).

22. WA, Tr 5, 95: #5362.

23. *Scriptorum publice propositorum a gvbernatoribus studiorum in Academia VVittenbergensi Tomus Tertius, Complectens annum 1556 et tres sequentes* (Wittenberg, 1559), pp. 190ᵇ–191ᵃ.

24. Otto Scheel, *Dokumente zu Luthers Entwicklung, bis 1519* (Tübingen: Mohr, 1911), #12, p. 19.

25. WA, Br 2, 76, 13.

26. WA, Br 2, 221, 18; Br 8, 619, 3 and E.

27. WA, Br 2, 221, 18; Br 5, 55, 11; Br 8, 327, 13; Br 9, 423, 7.

28. WA, Tr 3, 51: #2888 a and b.

29. WA, Tr 5, 255: #5573; Tr 5, 558: #6250.

30. WA, Br 2, 221, 18: #355.

31. WA, Br 3, 531, 23; Br 3, 538, 8; Br 3, 541, 10.

32. WA, Br 4, 95, 7: #1022.

33. *Scriptorum publice propositorum*, 3 (1559), p. 190ᵇ.

34. *CR*, 6, 156.

35. *Scriptorum publice propositorum*, 3 (1559), p. 190ᵇ.

36. WA, Tr 1, 551: #1101 erroneously gives 30 May, rather than 30 June 1531.

37. WA, Br 6, 103–106: #1820.

NOTES TO CHAPTER 2

1. H. E. Jacobs, *Martin Luther, The Hero of the Reformation 1483–1546* (New York: G. P. Putnam's Sons; London: Knickerbocker, 1902), p. 7.

2. WA 48, 249. See above, p. 12.

3. CR 6, 156.

4. Johannes Cochlaeus, *Commentaria Ioannis Cochlaei, de actis et scriptis Martini Lutheri Saxonis, Chronographicae, Ex ordine ab Anno Domini M. D. XVII, usque ad Annum M. D. XLVI. Inclusive, fideliter conscripta* (Mainz, 1549), Alᵃ; Paul Eber, *Calendarium historicum* (Wittenberg, 1556), 380; Simon Fontaine, *Historicae ecclesiasticae nostri temporis libri XVII* (Cologne, 1558), I. 380; Johann Mathesius, *Historien/von des Ehrwirdigen in Gott Seligen thewren Mann Gottes/ Doctoris Martini Luthers/anfang/lehr/leben und sterben* (Nürnberg,

1566), Predigt I, p. 1ª; reprinted in Georg Loesche, ed., *Johannes Mathesius, Ausgewählte Werke* (Prague, 1906), 3.12.

5. *Scriptorum publice propositorum*, 3 (1559), p. 190ᵇ.

6. Eberhard Matthes, "Luthers mütterliche Abstammung und Verwandtschaft: Margarethe Lindemann und ihre Sippe," *Archiv für Sippenforschung und alle verwandten Gebiete*, 12 (1935): 147.

7. J. K. F. Knaake, "Luthers Mutter eine geb. Ziegler," *Theologische Studien und Kritiken*, 54 (1881): 684–92.

8. *Scripta pvblice proposita a Professoribus in Academia Vuitebergensi ab anno 1540. usq³ ad annum 1553* (Wittenberg, 1553), Ciii a–b; cited by Knaake, "Luthers Mutter," pp. 689–90.

9. Veit Ludwig von Seckendorff, *Commentarius Historicus et Apologeticus de Lutheranismo sive De Reformatione Religionis ductu D. Martini Lutheri in magna Germanicae parte aliisque regionibus, et speciatum in Saxonia recepta et stabilita* (Frankfurt and Leipzig, 1692), Lib. 1, Sect. 8, 17, 20.

10. Wilhelm Ernst Tentzel, *Historiographi Saxoni, Historischer Bericht vom Anfang und erster Fortgang der Reformation Lutheri, Zur Erläuterung des Hn. v. Seckendorff Historie des Luthertums*, foreword and notes hy D. Ernst Salomon Cyprian, 2 vols. 2d impression (Leipzig, 1717), I, 139.

11. Tentzel-Cyprian, *Bericht*, p. 140 note.

12. Matthes, "Luthers mütterliche Abstammung," pp. 212–13; Knaake, "Luthers Mutter," p. 686.

13. *WA*, Br 5, 286, 26; Br 5, 407, 80; Br 6, 270, 9–16: #1908; *WA* 48, 252; Matthes, "Luthers mütterliche Abstammung," pp. 150–51.

14. Melanchthon in *CR* 6, 157.

15. Cyriac Spangenberg, *Die XV. Predigt. Von dem Getrewen Diener Jesu Christi/Doctore Martino Luthero/Wie er auff unsers HERRN GOTTES Berge eingefaren/getrecket/und andere notwendige arbeit verrichtet. Gethan in Thal Manszfeldt/1570. 19. Februarii* (Eisleben, 1571), pp. 5–6; quoted in Knaake, "Luthers Mutter," p. 691.

16. *ADB*, 35, pp. 37–41.

17. *WA*, Br 5, 354: #1586; Br 9, 334: #3579; *WA* 54, 487–96.

18. Knaake, "Luthers Mutter," p. 691.

19. Julius Köstlin, *Martin Luther: Sein Leben und Seine Schriften* 5th rev. edition, ed. Gustav Kawerau (Berlin: Duncker, 1903), 1, p. 13; Boehmer, *Road to Reformation* (Philadelphia: Fortress Press, 1946), p. 4.

20. Wilhelm Germann, *D. Johann Forster, der Hennebergische Reformator* (also containing *Urkunden zur Hennebergischen Kirchengeschichte*) (Meinigen, 1894), p. 400.

21. Germann, *Urkunden*, XV/1, pp. 22–23, n. 1.

22. Heinrich Boehmer, "Möhra (Zum 10. November)," *Allgemeine Evangelisch-Lutherische Kirchenzeitung*, 59 (1926): 1060–64, 1087–91, 1111–13.

23. Seckendorff, *Commentarius . . . de Lutherismo*, Lib. 1, Sect. 8, 20, Additio 1.

24. Boehmer, "Möhra," p. 1062.

25. WA, Br 5, 287–88, n. 14.

26. Matthes, "Luthers mütterliche Abstammung," pp. 146–51, 180–84, 212–17.

27. Quoted in Matthes, "Luthers mütterliche Abstammung," p. 182.

28. Ludwig Enders, "Ungedruckte Briefe Melanchthons an Georg Karg," *Beiträge zur bayerischen Kirchengeschichte*, 19 (1913): 142.

29. Quoted in Matthes, "Luthers mütterliche Abstammung," p. 183.

30. *De M. Cyriaco Lindemanno Oratio a. M. Iohanne Dinckelio*, ed. Cyr. Snegassius (Erfurt, 1593); cited in Matthes, "Luthers mütterliche Abstammung," pp. 182–83.

31. Cyriac Spangenberg, *Mansfeldische Chronica* (Eisleben, 1572), 4/1, pp. 361–64.

32. Heinrich Bornkamm, "Nachwort: Heinrich Boehmers 'Junger Luther' und die neuere Lutherforschung," in Boehmer, *Der junge Luther*, 2d ed. (Leipzig: Koehler, 1939), pp. 358–60.

NOTES TO CHAPTER 3

1. *ADB*, 37, pp. 286–87, signed "Reusch"; N. Paulus, "Petrus Sylvius. Ein katholischer Schriftsteller der Reformationszeit," *Der Katholik: Zeitschrift für katholische Wissenschaft und kirchliches Leben*, 3d series, 7 (1893): 49–67; Johann Karl Seidemann, "M. Petrus Sylvius, ein Dominicaner der Reformationszeit," *Archiv für Literaturgeschichte*, 4, no. 2 (1874): 117–53; K. Seidemann, "Die Schriften des Petrus Sylvius," ibid. 5, no. 1 (1875): 6–32; 5, no. 3 (1876): 287–310.

2. Petrus Sylvius, *Die Letzen zwey besch-/lissliche und aller krefftigste büch-leyn M. Petri Sylvii, so das Lutherisch thun an seyner per-son, von seyner geburt, und an seyner schrifft, von anfang/bis zum*

end gründlich handeln, und seyne unchrist-/ligkeit schrifftlich ent-
plossen (Leipzig, 1534), pp. Eiii ff., translated in part from Seidemann,
"Die Schriften des Petrus Sylvius," pp. 300–301, and in part from
Paulus, "Petrus Sylvius," pp. 61–62.

3. Sylvius, *Zwey newgedruckte nützlichste/büchlein, Aus welchen
das Erste handelt, von der gmeynen Christlichen kirchen, und/
mechtig-lich erklert./u.s.w.—Das ander büchlein handelt von/der
ungewöhnlichen Evangelischen kirchen, davon sich/die Pickarden
felschlisch Evangelisch nennen, und/das Evangelium nach irem mut-
willen gantz/böslich deuten und auslegen* (Leipzig, 1533), pp. Fiii ff.,
translated from Seidemann, "Die Schriften des Petrus Sylvius," p.
298.

4. Georg Witzel, *De raptu epistolae privatae, et praefixi illi,
criminatione, Contra Ludum Syl. Hessi. Expostulatio cum Hoste Iona.
Georg. Vuicelius Anno M.D. XXXV.* (n.p., but gives Erfurt, 1532 as
date of letter, Eisleben, October 1534 as date of preface), p. Cvi[a-b].

5. Johannes Luther, "Über Martin Luthers Vorfahren," *Luther:
Vierteljahrsschrift der Luthergesellschaft*, 15 (1933): 74.

6. Paul Bachmann (Amnicola), *Ein Maulstreich/dem Lutherischen
lügenhafftigen weyt auffge/spertem Rachen, das Clo-/sterleben zule-
stern und schenden./ Itzlichem Christlicher war/heit liebhaben,
nützlich zu le/sen./P.A.C./M.D.XXXIIII.* (Dresden, 1534), fol. B[a],
quoted in Otto Clemen, "Paul Bachmann, Abt von Altzelle," *Neues
Archiv für Sächsische Geschichte und Altertumskunde*, 26 (1905):
30.

7. Johannes Cochlaeus, *Hertzog Georgens zu Sachssen Ehrlich und
grundtliche ent-schuldigung/wider Martin Luthers Auffrüerisch und
verlo-genne/Brieff und Verant-wortung* (Dresden 1533), p. Aiii.

8. *WA*, Tr 3, 293, 6; 19: #3367 a and b.

9. *WA*, Tr 3, 650, 3–4: #3838.

10. *WA* 53, 511, 28–33.

11. *Nuntiaturbericht aus Deutschland 1533–1559. Bd I: Nuntiatu-
ren des Vergerio 1533–1536*, ed. Walter Friedensburg (Gotha, 1892),
pp. 541, 14–18.

12. Cochlaeus, *Commentaria*, Praefatio, p. Ciiii.

13. Adolf Herte, *Das katholische Lutherbild im Bann der Luther-
kommentare des Cochläus*, 3 vols. (Münster: Aschendorff, 1943). See
especially vol. 1, pp. 55–56, 60, 76–77, 119, 150, 169, 228 and n.;
and vol. 3, pp. 44, 89 and n.

14. Gabriel Dupréau (Prateolus), *De vitis, sectis, et dogmatibus
omnium haereticorum, qui ab orbe condito, ad nostra usque tem-*

pora, & veterum & recentum authorum monumentis proditi sunt, *ELENCHVS ALPHABETICVS* (Cologne: Calenius & Quentel, 1569), Book 10, 15: 271.

15. *ADB*, 42, pp. 266–70; Kurt Baschwitz, *Hexen und Hexenprozesse* (München: Rütten Loening, 1963), pp. 117–39; E. William Monter, ed., *European Witchcraft* (New York: Wiley, 1969), pp. 37–47; J. J. Cobben, *Jan Wier, Devils, Witches and Magic,* trans. Sal A. Prins (Ardmore, Pa.: Dorrance & Co., 1976); Dutch original: *Johannes Wier* (Assen, 1960).

16. Johann Wier, *Von Zauberey . . .* (n.p., 1566), 67ᵇ.

17. Wier, *de PRAESTIGIIS DAEMONVM, et incantationibus ac veneficiis Libres sex* (Basel, 1568), Book 3, chap. 24, pp. 302–4.

18. Herte, *Das katholische Lutherbild,* vol. 1, p. 8.

19. *ADB*, 23, pp. 257–61.

20. Johannes Nas, *Quinta centuria, das ist fünfft hundert, der Evangelischen wahrheit darin mit fleiss beschriben wirdt . . .* (Ingolstadt, 1570).

21. Nas, *Quinta centuria,* 29ᵛ–32ᵛ.

22. See Ernst Zeeden, *Martin Luther und die Reformation im Urteil des deutschen Luthertums* (Freiburg: Herder, 1950–52) vol. 2, pp. 15–16, 65; Hans-Jürgen Schönstädt, *Antichrist, Weltheilgeschehen und Gottes Werkzeug* (Wiesbaden: Steiner, 1978), p. 254.

23. See, for example, Johannes Herolt, O.P. (Discipulus), *Sermones Discipuli de tempore* 10. 1–5, the edition used here is that printed in Strassburg: [M. Flach], 1492, e5ᵃ–e6ᵇ (Hain 8503); anon., *Sermones thesauri novi, de tempore* 9.7, the edition used here is that printed at Strassburg: printer of the Vitaspatrum, 1483 (Copinger-Reichling 5410); Johann Gritsch, O.M., *Quadragesimale* 6.1, the edition used here is that printed at Ulm: Joh. Zainer, 1475 (Hain 8063).

24. On the significance of these calculations, especially the 1488 *Praktik* of the neoplatonic astrologer Lichtenberger, see Will-Erich Peuckert, *Die Grosse Wende: Das Apokalyptische Saeculum und Luther* (Darmstadt: Wissenschaftliche Buchgesellschaft, 1966), vol. 1, pp. 613–19.

25. See Mark U. Edwards, Jr., *Luther and the False Brethren* (Stanford: Stanford University Press, 1975).

26. *WA* 50, 601, 5–6; Br 5, 162: #1480; Tr 3, 620: #3795; *CR* 24, 64; *CR* 25, 80.

27. Article 17, On Monastic Vows, in *The Book of Concord,* ed. Theodore G. Tappert (Philadelphia: Fortress Press, 1959), pp. 268–69.

28. Carolus Gottlob Hoffman, *Memoriam saecularem Funeris et Sepulcri D. Martini Lutheri* (Wittenberg: Ahlfeld, 1746), p. 142.

29. Hoffmann, *Memoriam*, p. 106.

NOTES TO CHAPTER 4

1. Boehmer, "Möhra," *Allgemeine Evangelisch-Lutherische Kirchenzeitung*, 59 (1926): 1062.

2. Matthes, "Luthers mütterliche Abstammung und Verwandtschaft," *Archiv für Sippenforschung und alle verwandte Gebiete*, 12 (1935): 183.

3. *WA*, Br 5, 287, n. 14; Matthes, "Luthers mütterliche Abstammung," pp. 149–50.

4. *WA*, Br 5, 287, n. 14; Matthes, "Luthers mütterliche Abstammung," pp. 150–51.

5. Jacobs, *Martin Luther, The Hero of the Reformation, 1483–1546* (New York: G. P. Putnam's Sons, 1902), p. 7.

6. Kuiper, *Martin Luther: The Formative Years* (Grand Rapids, Mich.: Eerdmans, 1933), p. 16.

7. Lindsay, *Luther and the German Reformation* (Edinburgh: Clark, 1908), p. 12.

8. Ibid., p. 11.

9. *WA* 8, 573, 24.

10. *CR* 6, 156.

11. Ibid.

12. Boehmer, "Möhra," p. 1090.

13. Jerome Bruner, "Learning How to Do Things with Words," in *Human Growth and Development*, ed. J. Bruner and A. Garton (Oxford: Clarendon Press, 1978), p. 65.

14. Erik H. Erikson, *Young Man Luther: A Study in Psychoanalysis and History* (New York: W. W. Norton & Co., Inc., 1958), p. 72.

15. *CR* 6, 156.

16. *WA*, Br 1, 610, 20–25: #239.

17. *WA*, Tr 5, 95: #5362.

18. Martin Kessler, "Die Ahnen der Ursula Schweicker geb. Cotta in Eisenach," *Genealogie*, 7 (May–June 1964): 113–20. The information given in *WA*, Br 9, 549: #3687; Tr 6, 265, note 1: #6910; and Eberhard Matthes, *Das Eisenacher Lutherhaus* (Eisenach, 1939), Anhang: "Das Geschlecht Cotta," p. 61, must thus be corrected.

19. *WA*, Tr 5, 95: #5362; *WA* 30/3, 491, 37.

20. *WA*, Tr 6, 265, 2–4: #6910.

21. Matthes, "Luthers mütterliche Abstammung," p. 217.

22. *CR* 6, 156.

23. *Scriptorum publice propositorum,* 3 (1559), 190^b.

24. Boehmer, *Der junge Luther,* p. 24.

25. *WA,* Br 1, 10–11: #3.

26. See Leonhard Lemmens, "Der Franziskaner Johannes Hilten," *Römische Quartalschrift für christliche Altertumskunde und für Kirchengeschichte,* 37 (1929): 315–47.

27. Paul Johansen, "Johann von Hilten in Livland," *Archiv für Reformationsgeschichte,* 36, no. 1–2 (1939): 24–50.

28. *WA* 30/3, 491, 32–39.

29. *WA,* Br 1, 10 and 15: #3 and 5.

30. *WA,* Tr 1, 44: #116; Tr 3, 598: #3767; Mathesius, *Historien,* Predigt 1 (Loesch 3.18).

NOTES TO CHAPTER 5

1. David C. Steinmetz, *Luther and Staupitz: An Essay in the Intellectual Origins of the Reformation* (Durham, N.C.: Duke University Press, 1981).

2. *WA* 54, 179, 11 (a reference to Ovid, *Metamorphoses* 1. 7).

3. The phrase is borrowed from Natalie Davis, "Some Tasks and Themes in the Study of Popular Religion," *The Pursuit of Holiness,* ed. C. Trinkaus and H. Oberman (Leiden: Brill, 1974), p. 309.

4. Steven Ozment, *The Reformation in the Cities: The Appeal of Protestantism to Sixteenth-Century Germany and Switzerland* (New Haven: Yale University Press, 1975).

5. Thomas Tentler, *Sin and Confession on the Eve of the Reformation* (Princeton: Princeton University Press, 1977).

6. Johannes Herolt, O.P. ("Discipulus"), *Sermones de sanctis* (1434), prologue. The edition used here is that printed in Strassburg: [M. Flach], 1492, M 1^r.

7. The relevant numbers in Hain's *Repertorium Bibliographicum* and its supplements by Copinger and Reichling are as follows: *Gritsch:* Hain 8057–8082, Copinger 2800, Reichling 201, 1221; *Verdena:* Hain 15955–15979, Copinger 5971–5978, Reichling 356; *Sermones thesauri novi:* Copinger 5409–5438, Reichling 1390, suppl. 177; *Herolt:* Hain 8473–8522, Copinger 2921–2939, Reichling 207, 549, 1223, 1536, 1750.

8. Johannes Trithemius (Tritheim), *De scriptoribus ecclesiasticis* (Basel: Amerbach, 1494); Hain-Copinger 15613.

9. On these, see John O'Malley, *Praise and Blame in Renaissance*

Rome: Rhetoric, Doctrine & Reform in the Sacred Orators of the Papal Court, c1450–1521 (Durham, N.C.: Duke University Press, 1979).

10. See especially H. Caplan, *Medieval artes praedicandi: A Hand-List* (Ithaca, N.Y.: Cornell University Press, 1934); Th.-M. Charland, *Artes praedicandi: contribution à l'histoire de la rhétorique au moyen âge* (Ottawa: Institute d'études médiévales d'Ottawa, 1936); R. Cruel, *Geschichte der deutschen Predigt im Mittelalter* (Detwold: Meyer, 1879); A. Lecoy de la Marche, *La chaire française au moyen âge* (Paris: Renouard, 1886); G. R. Owst, *Preaching in Medieval England* (Cambridge: University Press, 1933); Ray Petry, *No Uncertain Sound: Sermons That Shaped the Pulpit Tradition* (Philadelphia: Westminster Press, 1948); Dorothea Roth, *Die mittelalterliche Predigttheorie und das Manuale Curatorum des Johann Ulrich Surgant* (Basel: von Helbing & Lichtenbahn, 1956); Anscar Zawart, *The History of Franciscan Preaching and of Franciscan Preachers 1209–1927, A Bio-bibliographical Study*, Franciscan Studies, 7 (New York: Wagner, 1928).

11. Johannes de Verdena (Werden), O.M., *Sermones dormi secure*, preface. The edition used here is that printed at Nürnberg: A. Koberger, 1498; Hain-Copinger 15977.

12. Herolt, *Sermones de sanctis*, M 1^r.

13. See Harry Caplan, "The Four Senses of Scriptural Interpretation and the Mediaeval Theory of Preaching," *Speculum*, 4 (July 1929):282–90; Beryl Smalley, *The Study of the Bible in the Middle Ages* (Oxford: Clarendon Press, 1941).

14. F. R. Goff, "The Postilla of Guillermus Parisiensis," *Gutenberg Jahrbuch*, 34 (1959): 73–78.

15. *The Book of Margery Kempe, 1436*; a modern version by W. Butler-Bowdon, with an introduction by R. W. Chambers (London: Jonathan Cape, 1936).

16. Vincenz Hasak, *Dr. M. Luther und die religiöse Literatur seiner Zeit bis zum Jahre 1520* (Regensburg: Manz, 1881; reprint ed. Nieuwkoop: de Graaf, 1967), pp. 27–28.

17. *WA* 38, 105, 8; cf. Tr 6, 238: #6859. The fact of Duke Wilhelm of Anhalt's early death was disputed by Johann Cochlaeus when he read Luther's account.

18. Werden, *Sermones dormi secure, de tempore*, 11.2.

19. Ibid., 57.1.

20. Ibid., 15.3.

21. *Sermones thesauri novi*, 24,0. This anonymous collection ∙ is wrongly attributed in many catalogues to Petrus de Palude, O.P. (d.

1342), more plausibly attributed by some to Petrus de Colle, O.M. (fl. 1440). It is plainly a mid fifteenth-century collection, since it cites Lyra, Herolt, and a canon of the Council of Basel. The edition used here is that printed at Strassburg: printer of the Vitaspatrum, 1483; Copinger-Reichling 5410.

22. Gritsch, *Quadragesimale,* sermon 10. The edition used here is that printed at Ulm: Joh. Zainer, 1475; Hain 8063: viii, O.

23. *Quadragesimale,* sermon 31; xxx,D.

24. Herolt, *Sermones de tempore,* 115.O(E).

25. Otto Scheel, *Dokumente zu Luthers Entwicklung,* no. 12, p. 19.

26. *WA, Tr* 1, 46: #119 and notes.

27. *WA* 40/1, 315, 2.

28. *CR* 6, 158.

29. *WA, Tr* 4, 440: #4707.

30. Herolt, *Sermones de tempore,* 108.2(S) ·

31. Ibid., 87.1(E).

32. *Sermones thesauri novi,* 134, D–E.

33. Herolt, *Sermones de tempore,* 71.3(T).

34. Ibid., 102.22(L).

35. Gritsch, *Quadragesimale,* Monday in Holy Week, xl,N.

36. Herolt, *Sermones de tempore,* 97.3(E).

37. Werden, *Sermones dormi secure, de tempore,* 6.2.

38. Ibid., 12.0.

39. Ibid., 17.1,2.

40. *WA* 37, 274, 14.

NOTES TO CHAPTER 6

1. Ernst Zeeden, *The Legacy of Luther: Martin Luther and the Reformation in the Estimation of the German Lutherans from Luther's Death to the Beginning of the Age of Goethe,* trans. Ruth M. Bethel (London: Hollis & Carter, 1954), p. xi. German original: *Martin Luther und die Reformation im Urteil des deutschen Luthertums,* vol. 1 (Freiburg: Herder, 1950).

2. Jaroslav J. Pelikan, *Luther the Expositor: Introduction to the Reformer's Exegetical Writings,* companion volume to *Luther's Works,* American Edition (St. Louis: Concordia Publishing House, 1959), pp. 33–34.

3. Roland H. Bainton, *Here I Stand: A Life of Martin Luther* (Nashville, Tenn.: Abingdon Press, 1950).

4. E. Gordon Rupp, "Luther: The Contemporary Image," in *The*

Church, Mysticism, Sanctification and the Natural in Luther's Thought, ed. Ivar Asheim (Philadelphia: Fortress Press, 1967), p. 19.

5. Erik H. Erikson, *Young Man Luther: A Study in Psychoanalysis and History* (New York: W. W. Norton & Co., Inc., 1958), pp. 65, 255.

6. Ibid., p. 255.

7. Ibid., pp. 71–73.

8. See, e.g., Lewis W. Spitz, "Psychohistory and History: The Case of Young Man Luther," *Soundings,* 56, no. 2 (Summer 1973): 1956; reprinted in Roger A. Johnson, ed., *Psychohistory and Religion: The Case of Young Man Luther* (Philadelphia: Fortress Press, 1977); Heinrich Bornkamm, *Luther: Gestalt und Wirkungen* (Gütersloh: Mohn, 1975), p. 22; Roland H. Bainton, "Luther und seine Mutter," *Luther: Zeitschrift der Luther-Gesellschaft,* 44, no. 3 (1973): 123ff.

9. See, e.g., WA 20, 148, 26ff.; Tr 1, 531–32: #1054; TR 3, 25–26: #2847 a and b.

10. See Maria Grossmann, *Humanism in Wittenberg 1485–1517* (Nieuwkoop: De Graaf, 1975), p. 59.

11. WA 10/2, 293, 8–10; 53, 421, 7–14; Tr 3, 3: #2807b. cf. Tr 2, 166: #1658; Tr 3, 378: #3528.

12. See, for instance, the treatment of Rebecca in WA 43, 329 ff. and 498 ff.

13. Erikson, *Young Man Luther,* p. 71.

14. WA 7, 572, 28.

15. Karl Holl, "Luthers Urteile über sich selbst" (1903), in his *Gesammelte Aufsätze zur Kirchengeschichte. I, Luther,* 7th ed. (Tübingen: Mohr [Siebeck], 1948), p. 382. A good English translation by H. C. Erik Midelfort, "Martin Luther on Luther," may be found in *Interpreters of Luther: Essays in Honor of Wilhelm Pauck,* ed. Jaroslav Pelikan (Philadelphia: Fortress Press, 1968), pp. 9–34.

16. WA 43, 414, 2 and 6.

17. WA 43, 345, 9 and 28 and 33; cf. 44, 327, 2.

18. WA 54, 32, 22–24.

19. WA 10/1/1. 131, 1–2.

20. WA DB 7, 10, 9.

21. WA 17/2. 106, 11–12.

22. WA 39/1, 46, 3–4.

23. WA 21, 488, 1–2, 16–17.

24. WA 10/1/1. 484, 14–15.

25. WA 10/3, 285, 24–28.

26. WA 42, 452, 17, 22–23.

27. WA 40/1, 233, 4, 18.

28. WA 7, 547, 8; 549, 29.

29. WA 7, 550, 5–13.

30. Ian D. K. Siggins, *Martin Luther's Doctrine of Christ* (New Haven, Conn.: Yale University Press, 1970), pp. 156–64.

31. WA, Tr 5, 412: #5966.

32. Siggins, *Luther's Doctrine of Christ*, pp. 39–47, 137–43, 172–90, 247–49.

33. WA 10/1/1, 280, 11 ff.; Siggins, *Luther's Doctrine of Christ*, pp. 251–52.

34. WA 45, 154, 1.

35. WA 40/1, 167, 24; 18, 141, 12; Siggins, *Luther's Doctrine of Christ*, p. 265.

36. WA 10/1/2, 430, 36.

37. WA 13, 508, 16.

38. WA 45, 679, 16.

39. WA 30/2, 272–73; 370–71; 404.

40. WA 30/2, 580–81.

41. WA 46, 100, 7.

42. WA 45, 679, 22.

43. WA 31/2, 405, 1.

Index

93